A Manual of Graphology

ERIC SINGER

ERIC SINGER

A Manual of Graphology

WITH DRAWINGS BY
GERTRUDE ELIAS

CRESCENT BOOKS
New York

The three individual titles comprising this book were originally
published as follows:

Graphology for Everyman: First published in Great Britain in 1949
The Graphologist's Alphabet: First published in Great Britain in 1950
A Handwriting Quiz Book: First published in Great Britain in 1953

These three titles first published together in Great Britain as one
volume under the title *A Manual of Graphology* in 1969 and reprinted
in 1974

This edition published in the United
States by Crescent Books, distributed by
Crown Publishers, Inc.
by arrangement with Octopus Books Limited

Printed in Czechoslovakia

ISBN 0–517–61672–6

FOREWORD

MY husband Eric Singer, a Doctor of Law
of Vienna University, studied handwriting
analysis and psychology under experts in
Austria and Switzerland. He specialized in English
handwritings and worked in London as consulting
graphologist. When he died, eight years ago, he left
behind him three popular books on graphology:
Graphology for Everyman, The Graphologist's Alphabet
and *A Handwriting Quiz Book.* The first went through
three impressions, and the others have been altogether
out of print for some time.

In view of the continued interest in graphology
everywhere—in Britian this interest was certainly due
largely to my husband's own treatment of the subject
at a popular level—I have decided, in consultation with
the publisher, to reissue these three books all together
under a new title, *A Manual of Graphology.* All Mrs.
Gertrude Elias's amusing sketches, so original a feature
of these books, have been retained, and only such
editing of the combined text has been done as will
eliminate unnecessary repetition.

I commend this comprehensive *Manual* to a new
generation of students of this ever fascinating subject.

E. A. SINGER

London 1969

CONTENTS

PART ONE

GRAPHOLOGY FOR EVERYMAN

GENERAL INTRODUCTION

FOR many hundreds of years society has recognized the fact that the handwritten signature of a human being is something unmistakable, unique, personal and individual. It is asked for as an acknowledgment of the receipt of goods and money, and it is necessary to make some kinds of legal agreement valid. If you make an affidavit for a court of law, you confirm it with your signature. By writing your signature on a cheque, you dispose of your own money. To forge another person's signature is a crime heavily punished by the criminal law of every country.

By giving the features of your handwriting such protection, society recognizes it as an identification of your individual character and personality. In normal social life too, it is a common experience for all of us, particularly those who have a fairly good visual memory, to recognize the individual handwriting of friends and relations and to distinguish one handwriting from another.

So it is not surprising that, from earliest times, many famous people have tried to deduce from the appearance of a man's handwriting an impression of the writer's personality. Suetonius, the Roman historian, always noted the particular characteristics of the handwriting of the emperor whose biography he was writing. Many great men, amongst them famous writers like Shakespeare, Byron, Walter Scott, Browning and the American Edgar Allan Poe, have tried, in an amateur and intuitive way, to discover the relationship between the handwriting and character of a person.

9

In spite of all this, in spite of the old natural popular belief that there must be some connection between handwriting and character, how does it happen that' graphology, the art and science of studying a human being's character from his handwriting, is either

  completely unknown, or

  mistaken for something different, or

  regarded with suspicion by so many.

For each of these three attitudes there are, of course, reasons. The lack of information about graphology is simply due to the fact that it is still a young science. It was not till 1875 that the French abbot and novel-writer, Hippolyte Michon, the acknowledged father of modern graphology, published his first book on the subject, and used the term graphology for the first time, a term which is now commonly accepted as denoting handwriting psychology. In spite of the many excellent books which have been written on the subject, grapho-logy has not yet—at least in this country—found its way to schools, universities, lecture-halls and news-papers, as have the other branches of psychology. Consequently, the number of learned professional ex-perts, research workers and teachers is still small, though larger in countries like France, Germany and Austria than in Holland and England. At the moment the outstanding research workers are in Switzerland, where already the common man takes considerable interest in the development of graphology.

As for the second attitude, it is a misconception to regard graphology as a kind of fortune-telling gypsy-practice, which can read into the future. The reason for this superstition is that some of the people who call themselves graphologists are, in fact, either charlatans or, sometimes, very gifted telepaths. Stimulated by the handwriting in a letter, they have genuine visions, sometimes very curious visions, of the writer's past, present and future and of the actual circumstances under which the letter was written.

Scientific graphology cannot tell whether the writer of a letter was sitting in a tent in the desert, or whether he was wearing a green tie, or whether he is dead or alive, as some of the outstanding telepaths can certainly do. Scientific graphology cannot foretell the future of the writer like the telepathic visionary. If it does make statements about the future of a person, it is only expressing a potentiality which arises from the study of the writer's present disposition and character. A person's potentiality naturally depends on future circumstances in his life. These, graphology can in no way foretell.

Concerning doubts about the genuine possibilities of reading character from handwriting, one has always to contend with the same arguments. These arguments have been extensively and thoroughly dealt with in most of the systematic theoretical books on graphology. Amongst the books written in English, R. Saudek's *Handwriting and Character* and H. J. Jacoby's *Analysis of Handwriting* both contain a comprehensive enumeration and refutation of all these arguments.

For the purposes of this book it is enough to deal with the three most important of them.

ARGUMENT I.

"There is no real difference between handwritings, as they are all formed according to text-book patterns learnt in school."

Let us take a simple case and see how far this argument goes. Take, for instance, the different ways in which the small "t" is formed, connected and crossed by different writers. To the writer himself, it may seem insignificant; but a look at samples 1 to 26 inclusive will show what astonishing variety there can be.

SAMPLE 1	*intention*	Crossing of the T overhead
SAMPLE 2	*not effectuer's*	Sometimes it just touches the top of the T
SAMPLE 3	*ptd*	T crossed at the normal "textbook" level
SAMPLE 4	*to*	T crossed below a normal level
SAMPLE 5	*entbish*	No crossing of the T at all
SAMPLE 6	*distinti*	Crossing of the T sloping upwards
SAMPLE 7	*tolerance*	Crossing of the T sloping downwards
SAMPLE 8	*written Lenten*	Crossing of the T "sharpening" at the end
SAMPLE 9	←	Crossing of the T broadening at the end
SAMPLE 10	*stamps*	Crossing of the T with a "hook" or "hooks"

SAMPLE 11	*Saltla*	T with a knot
SAMPLE 12	*Director,*	T with a loop in the middle of the downstroke
SAMPLE 13	*Oct*	T with a loop at the top or the bottom of the downstroke
SAMPLE 14A	*stories,*	T with cross-stroke on the left
SAMPLE 14B	*post,*	T with cross-stroke on the right
SAMPLE 15	*set, at ot*	T with a triangle ending with a horizontal stroke
SAMPLE 16		T crossed with a loop bending upwards and backwards to the left
SAMPLE 17		T crossed with a loop bending downwards and backwards to the right
SAMPLE 18	*talk*	T crossed with a wavy line

SAMPLE 19   *to*   *the*   T formed like a " printed character "

SAMPLE 20   *attin*   T with both a knot and cross

SAMPLE 21   *for overprinted*   T crossed and the cross connected with the next letter or the dot of an " i "

SAMPLE 22   *nexY*   T inverted

SAMPLE 23   *motine*   *dentc*   T with the cross going backwards and overhead

SAMPLE 24A   *to day started*   T crossed roofs the whole word

SAMPLE 24B   *statt fes.*   or even connects several words

SAMPLE 25   *Statements etc.*   T like musical key or notes

SAMPLE 26   *getir,.*   T cross stroke instead of whole letter

14

In a sample of handwriting you may come across several different types of T, but when a writer sticks to one particular form you can certainly draw conclusions from it. In any case, these T examples give the reader some idea of the differences which exist between individual handwritings. These differences occur not only in the case of T, but in all the other letters of the alphabet. But, as the reader will soon observe, more important than the differences between single letters, are the differences in the general tendencies of handwriting viz. direction, connection, size, spacing, etc.

ARGUMENT II. *"Everybody changes his handwriting even during a single day just according to his varying mood and disposition. How can his basic character be revealed by such a changing barometer?"*

In fact, the changing elements in handwriting only represent a small proportion of the whole. The basic features always remain the same, and change only when the character of the individual undergoes a real change. Interesting experiments in hypnosis have confirmed this statement. In the cases where the hypnotized person is asked to assume another character, the characteristics of his handwriting also change immediately. If he is asked to be an emperor, he will write with all the pomp and majesty, which he thinks is typical of the handwriting of a ruler. If asked to be a child, he will write with all the unskilled effort of an infant scribe.

What are the basic features of handwriting which I referred to earlier in this chapter? They can be grouped in the following way:

I SIZE
Large writing (see Sample 16, 29).
Normal size writing (see Sample 22).
Small writing (see Sample 27).

SAMPLE 27

SAMPLE 28

SAMPLE 29

DRAFT

SAMPLE 30

SAMPLE 31

Karte gemacht hat

SAMPLE 32

SAMPLE 33

SAMPLE 34

trotz grösster Bemühungen, nicht

SAMPLE 35

SAMPLE 36

SAMPLE 37

Hugh

SAMPLE 38

I am most annoyed to learn

SAMPLE 40

SAMPLE 39

SAMPLE 41

Kindest

SAMPLE 42

16

Size of words increasing (see Sample 28).
Size of words decreasing (see Sample 29).
Proportionate lengths of small letters (e.g. *m*, *n*, etc.), Medium-size letters (e.g. *l*, *g*, *h*, etc.) and the tall letters (e.g. *f*), varying.

In the study of the proportionate length of letters, the graphologist has to think of three zones like the three equal spaces between the lines in a child's writing book. The small letters cover only the middle zone, the medium-size letters cover two zones, and the tall letters all three zones. The length of the strokes in each zone can be out of proportion, either too long or too short compared with the length of the strokes in the other zones (see Samples 3, 11, 34, 50, 99, 121).

II GENERAL LAYOUT. That is to say, the arrangement of the writing on the page, the character of the margin (e.g. broad, narrow, constant or varying distance between the edge of the page and the writing).

III DIRECTION OF LINES
Sloping upwards (see Samples 30, 64).
Sloping downwards (see Sample 33).
Curved in the form of an arc (see Sample 32).
Curved in the form of an inverted arc (see Sample 35).

IV DEGREE OF CONNECTION
Connected writing (see Samples 8, 12, 16).
Unconnected writing (see Sample 34).

We call it connected writing when at least four or five letters in one word are connected.. If a break is made by the writer merely to cross the *t* or dot the *i*, the lack of connection is not significant.

anything excitement

SAMPLE 43

SAMPLE 44

letters

SAMPLE 45

Amy Potts

SAMPLE 46

Lote

SAMPLE 47

SAMPLE 48

pushed

SAMPLE 49

SAMPLE 50

London.

SAMPLE 51

Mr. Singer.

SAMPLE 52

By all means.

SAMPLE 53

Singer

SAMPLE 54

Tam

SAMPLE 56

SAMPLE 55

SAMPLE 57

SAMPLE 58

SAMPLE 59

hier hom must

SAMPLE 60

V Form of Connection of Upstrokes and Downstrokes

According to the copybook (see Samples 6, 109).

In angular form (see Samples 38, 121).

Curved at the top only (*arcade* form) (see Samples 16, 66).

Curved at the bottom only (*garland* form) (see Samples 8, 40).

Curved at the top and bottom (wavy line) (see Samples 25, 34).

Degenerating into a thread-like stroke (see Samples 44, 55).

Each of the above forms of connection can be made by a so-called "covering stroke", that is the writer moves up again along the down stroke as far as the middle of the stroke before linking with the next stroke (see Sample 38).

VI Regularity

We call it regular writing (see Sample 45) when the size of small letters, the angle of writing and the distance between downstrokes are constant; irregular if not (see Sample 46).

VII Rhythm

We call it rhythmic writing when the tendency of the writing, whether regular or irregular, is maintained from the beginning to the end of the writing (see Sample 7). We call it arrhythmic if it changes in the course of the writing (see Sample 46). Some graphologists use the term "even" instead of "rhythmic" to describe this characteristic.

Marjan

SAMPLE 61

Maple

SAMPLE 62

vieleicht wird das ganze wieder aufgehoben. Es ist aus ganz gleich was

SAMPLE 63

much

SAMPLE 65

mmm

SAMPLE 66

Frisch fr

SAMPLE 64

Ditt z Eric

SAMPLE 67

slow

SAMPLE 68

I am sending you my bigger book; you won't read it, but you will feel you have got value for money. I am very glad to have yours, & I will see if I can't write a notice somewhere, & will see it gets a mention in the Annual Bulletin

SAMPLE 69

Lieben!

SAMPLE 70

attached

Songs.

SAMPLE 72

Verbindung

SAMPLE 71

SAMPLE 73

Correctiv

SAMPLE 74

an Westend

SAMPLE 76

immer

SAMPLE 75

for

SAMPLE 78 *Moar*

SAMPLE 77

VIII Degree of Broadness

Wide handwriting (see Sample 5).

Narrow handwriting (see Sample 31).

Handwriting is of normal width when the distance between two downstrokes is equal to the height of the writer's small letters (*e, m, n*, etc.).

IX Speed of Writing

Quick writing (see Sample 1).

Slow writing (see Sample 52).

The speed of handwriting can be ascertained by many characteristics about which Saudek has made very extensive studies. The principal signs of fast writing are when overstrokes (the dotting of the *i*, crossing of the *t*) begin to the right of the letter instead of over or through the letter, when the angle of the writing slopes to the right, and when the end strokes of the words are extended to the right. Other characteristics are garland connection and connected writing.

X Form of Letters

We use the term "simplified" when the form of the letter is reduced to the essential (see Sample 27). We call it "complicated", "enriched" or "amplified" when it is elaborated without spoiling the clarity of the form (see Sample 41). We call it "neglected" when the essentials are left out so that the whole writing becomes difficult to read (see Sample 44) and we call it "overloaded" or "flourishing" when the essentials of the letters are overshadowed by too many superfluous flourishes (see Sample 37).

SAMPLE 79

SAMPLE 80

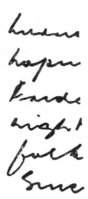

SAMPLE 81

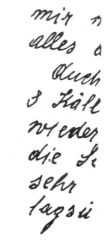

SAMPLE 82

SAMPLE 83

SAMPLE 84

XI Covering of Space

Full writing (see Sample 41).

Lean writing (see Sample 28).

Full writing is writing which takes up a lot of space for the number of lines written. The fullness is due to the fact that the strokes of the writing are more curved and rounded.

XII Shading of Writing

Distinct shading (see Sample 16).

This means thin upstrokes and strong downstrokes.

Pasty writing (see Sample 31).

In this writing the strokes are not sharp, but shaded, giving the impression that the writer has been using a brush.

As to pressure itself, we must also watch the degree applied in writing, also whether it is applied in a way emphasizing the downstrokes, or in the case of the upstrokes or connecting strokes, where, according to copybook handwriting, pressure is not called for.

In watching the shading in handwriting we must first try to find out what kind of pen has been used. The modern fountain-pen has a tendency to shade all handwriting and make the writing of clear thin strokes difficult if not impossible.

XIII Angle of the Writing

Upright (see Samples 12, 27, 41, 43).

Slanting to the right (see Samples 14, 20, 33, 37).

Slanting to the left (see Samples 8, 32).

The angle of handwriting is formed by the downstrokes and an imaginary horizontal line at the base of the letters.

SAMPLE 85

you an

it

SAMPLE 86

SAMPLE 88

SAMPLE 87

SAMPLE 90

SAMPLE 89

24

XIV RIGHT AND LEFT TENDENCIES

Left tendencies are shown not only by writing slanting to the left, but by end-strokes or upper strokes going back to the left (see Samples 16, 17).

XV SPACING

Between words.

Between lines.

Spacing can be distinct (Sample 40), exaggerated (Sample 27), or neglected (Sample 43). In neglected spacing, words in the same line are linked up and two lines of writing can either touch or even mingle.

XVI DEGREE OF ATTENTION

In this connection we must watch the beginning and end of words or lines, and the end of the page, also the writing of overstrokes, capital letters and concluding end-strokes. Under this heading special attention must be paid to the difference between writing an address, or a signature, and the rest of the writing.

ARGUMENT 3. *"Handwriting is produced by the movement of the hand only. Therefore differences in handwriting can only reveal skill, routine or deficiencies of the hand, but can tell nothing of the writer's character."*

This is contradicted by the hypnosis experiments already mentioned. The changes in the handwriting of a person under hypnotic influence have their origin in a changed conception of the writer about his own personality; the change springs from his brain and imagination and not from his hand.

There are other experiments, too, which have proved that the general features of handwriting remain the same whether a person writes with his hand, with his

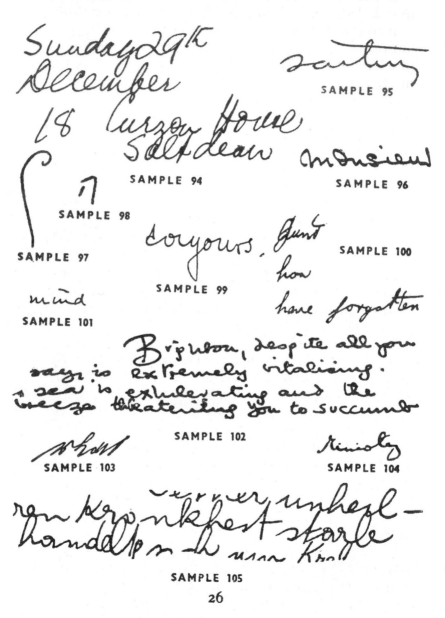

SAMPLE 91

SAMPLE 92

SAMPLE 93

SAMPLE 95

SAMPLE 94

SAMPLE 96

SAMPLE 98

SAMPLE 97

SAMPLE 100

SAMPLE 99

SAMPLE 101

SAMPLE 102

SAMPLE 103

SAMPLE 104

SAMPLE 105

26

foot, with his mouth, with the end of an umbrella or even with smoke in the sky. The writing is, of course, less skilled, less elaborate and less certain, but to the trained eye it is exactly the same and reveals the same unmistakable and characteristic details and tendencies (the kind of details that you have been reading about in the last few pages).

An interesting court case occurred in Germany about twenty years ago. A farmer was living on bad terms with his neighbour. To offend him he deliberately sowed seeds on his neighbour's field in the form of libellous words. The seeds grew to plants which were in the exact pattern of the offender's handwriting. The court accepted this as evidence and legal proof of the offender's identity, and he was convicted.

If handwriting is not merely the result of a movement of the hand, what is it then?

Among other things, it is certainly a movement of the hand (forearm and fingers) made with the writing instrument on the paper. It is put into motion by a motor activity of the left side of the brain. It has to overcome technical difficulties, such as the resistance of the paper and of the writing instrument and sometimes others, such as a wobbling table in a swaying train. The effect of the writing movement is controlled by the eyes.

The technical and physical pre-conditions of the actual writing will therefore be the first thing to be examined by the graphologist. The second will be the reconstruction of the movement itself and of the impression this movement conveys of the personality of the writer.

In so far as writing is a movement, the manuscript is its fixation on the paper. The fixing of this movement allows you to reconstruct in your mind the impressions which would be made on you by the habitual movements and gestures of the writer.

nice

SAMPLE 106

revd.

SAMPLE 107

SAMPLE 108

numbers

SAMPLE 109

3 U
count
Capt
Little
Stonno

SAMPLE 110

Suis

SAMPLE 111

7

SAMPLE 112

long

SAMPLE 113

flat

SAMPLE 114

Js

SAMPLE 115

A

SAMPLE 116

future,

SAMPLE 118

I hope

SAMPLE 119

Dear Docta

SAMPLE 120

I purchased

SAMPLE 121

Zürich

SAMPLE 122

Wh Treue

Nin w

Neus

Weil

SAMPLE 117

28

But writing is not an aimless movement. The writer has to work out a definite manuscript, and to overcome all the psychological, physical and intellectual difficulties which hinder this accomplishment. From this point of view, handwriting is work and gives you, therefore, an account of how the writer works, plans, arranges and overcomes difficulties. It will also tell you something of his standard of intelligence, memory, education, skill, energy, vitality, abilities and discipline.

From the purely graphological point of view, the text itself can be left out of our analysis. It is, however, interesting in two respects. Firstly, when certain words, and the thoughts connected with them, consistently make the writer stop, hasten, slip or make mistakes, then we can draw conclusions about the effect certain thoughts have on the writer. Secondly when comparing different manuscript texts written by the same writer, we may get an impression of which topics are brought to paper quickly, keenly and with interest and which are not. We can also draw conclusions when the writer leaves out words or repeats them.

Writing means also the production of letters, i.e. certain agreed copybook forms, and the transformation of these forms by each writer to similar ones with certain alterations. These alterations consist of two kinds of mostly unconscious activity: the omission of parts of the letters which the writer considers unpleasant, difficult to produce or unessential, and the addition or emphasis of other parts, which the writer feels to be pleasant, easy to form or important.

From this point of view handwriting is an expression of the writer's unconscious likes and dislikes, his tastes and his preferences. In so far as he imitates in the personal forming of his letters certain models and standards of other writers, an indication is given of where he looks for his heroes.

This movement of the hand, transforming the letters can go so far that the writer, by making painting gestures when writing, produces suggestions of pictures, but reduced to the basic outlines. These pictures will be those dominating his mind and his imagination at the time. So handwriting can also become the expression of imagery, a gallery of pictures drawn from the unconscious mind of the writer.

Writing is also the solving of a problem of space. Max Pulver, the Swiss graphologist, has formulated this fact clearly, and I offer his presentation herewith. The writer is faced by the empty paper which he has to fill. He has to start somewhere on the left, to work up and down and to go on to the right. Now it is inherent in human nature, and confirmed by the psychology of the unconscious, that every problem of form and space becomes symbolic in the individual's mind of his own position in the different spheres of space and time, that is to say, his spiritual, social and material world. And so the point along a line of writing at which the moving pen of a writer arrives becomes a symbol of his own position in the world around him; to the left of this point lies the past, origin, mother and childhood, to the right lies the work to be done, the future, the writer's fellow men and the social world. Movement upwards above the extension of the short letters (*m*, *n*, *u*, etc.) symbolizes gravitation towards spiritual and intellectual spheres; movement below symbolizes a dive into the material, sub-human and sub-conscious world. Thus the manuscript becomes a symbol of the writer's attitude to the past and the future, to himself and to others, to the spiritual, social and material world, to airy dreams and to sub-conscious impulses.

Writing is also the fitting of parts (letters and words) into a whole. This can be done easily or the writer may have to overcome considerable inner resistance by conflicting tendencies.   These conflicting handwriting tendencies reveal conflict in the writer. Apart from this real inner conflict, there may be a difference between the normal handwriting of the writer and certain manuscripts, or parts of manuscripts, of his which show that the writer has something he wants to disguise. We shall come back to some of these points in later chapters.

I am often asked whether you can learn graphology. The answer to this question is the same as in the case of all the sciences, which are in fact arts in practice, like psychology, medicine, etc. Yes, if you have a gift for it, if you are interested in it and ready to study hard. Like medicine and psychology, it cannot be learnt by books alone. Books are only useful when backed by basic instruction from an experienced graphologist, and by actual practice in graphology. Instruction, observation and experience are, in any case, necessary, in addition to the preliminary gifts of visual memory and observation, interest in handwriting, intuition, knowledge of human nature and both an analytical and synthetical mind. One of the main results of learning it from books alone is the judging of handwriting by a few signs picked up from the books. This always proves very misleading, as each writing tendency has many meanings and the character of the writer can only be judged by taking them all into account in a balanced way.

This book is, however, not a text-book of graphology. It does not presume to make a perfect handwriting psychologist of the reader. Its modest aim is to inform him, to awaken his interest and to give him the up-to-date facts, about what graphology means, its history, how it works, and where it can be applied.

CHAPTER II

THE HISTORY OF GRAPHOLOGY

THE first specialized book dealing with the relationship between handwriting and the character of the writer was published in 1622 in Capri by Camillo Baldi (Baldo), an Italian, who was both Doctor of Medicine and Philosophy and Professor of Theoretical Medicine at the University of Bologna. Another Italian professor, this time of Anatomy, called Marcus Aurelius Severinus, wrote a book on the same subject about the same time; but he died from the plague in 1656 before it was published. From the mid-seventeenth century onwards, the number of articles and treatises on this topic continued to increase. The most important of them are the studies of the Swiss physiognomist Lavater in the eighteenth century and a book by the French writer Hocquart which appeared in 1812, at first anonymously.

The real origins of modern graphology are to be found in France. A study circle formed amongst the members of the higher French clergy systematically examined the relationship between human qualities and their graphic expression in handwriting. Cardinal Regnier, Archbishop of Cambrai, Bishop Boudinet of Amiens and the Abbé Flandrin belonged to this study group. Flandrin later became the teacher of the man who is the acknowledged founder of modern graphology as a science, Jean Hippolyte Michon (1806–81); Michon also established the name Graphology which is composed of the Greek words grapho, meaning I write, and logos, which means theory or doctrine. The Abbé Michon, like most of the great graphological research workers before and after him, was a man of wide knowledge with many spheres of interest. In the course of his long life he published not only novels but also books on many topics; but the sphere in which he won the greatest success and everlasting fame was graphology, where he formulated almost all the signs and rules on which it is still based. Michon, who himself called graphology an art, worked only by experience and observation. In the course of years of study, he compared the handwriting of thousands of people whose character was familiar to him.· With his intuitive genius and great faculties of observation, he found the graphic signs which writers with similar qualities and deficiencies have in common. With the help of his collaborators, Delestre and Debarolle, he collected the signs of almost every human quality and published them from 1872 onwards. By his life work Michon produced an invaluable catalogue, so far unsurpassed, of graphological signs and rules based on his own experience. He did not attempt, however, to explain the probable reasons for the production of these signs, or to connect the psychology of handwriting with other branches of physiology or psychology, or to form a theoretical system.

The French school which followed him, led by his eminent pupil, Jules Crépieu-Jamin, continued to emphasize experience and empirical comparison in their graphological research. However, Crépieu-Jamin abandoned Michon's doctrine of definite signs, which point to only one meaning, and elaborated a more subtle system of co-ordination of dominant signs. A society for the study of graphology was founded by Depoin, who also edited a periodical. Thus a centre of research and discussion was created, which attracted many illustrious Frenchmen including Dr. Binet, Director of the Sorbonne, Arsène Aruss and G. Tarde the sociologist. This tradition is upheld by the modern French school.

The theoretical system of graphology, based on physiology and psychology and its connection with the other branches of characterology, was the work of the German school. In Germany a contemporary of Michon, Adolf Hentze, worked as a graphological practitioner for a Leipzig periodical and by a series of correct handwriting analyses not only thrilled the readers of the paper but also drew attention to the subject. The books and articles, however, which this writer published did not help the development of research, the impetus for which came from Austria. Here E. Schwiedland, later a Professor of Economics, published articles and a book based on the discoveries of the French school. Later, Schwiedland's interest was fully absorbed by economics, but his pupils, for instance, the gifted Austrian woman Rudolphine Poppée and the German Wilhelm Langenbruch, worked on so that the new science should be recognized. Langenbruch, a very able expert, founded in 1895 a periodical entirely devoted to graphology. He introduced two medical doctors to assist his researches and these later became his chief collaborators. One of them, Dr. William Preyer, a University Professor of Medical Physiology, was born in England. He went as a child to Germany and became the founder of the new theory which took into account the physiology, psychology and pathology of handwriting and so connected graphology with the other achievements of modern science.

In 1897, a second graphological periodical was founded in Germany, also a society for graphological research. The founder of both was Hans Busse, a gifted practitioner and an able organizer who edited a critical German edition of Crépieu-Jamin's main works. The chief contributors to Busse's periodical were Dr. Georg Meyer and Busse's assistant editor, Dr. Ludwig Klages. Dr. Georg Meyer was psychiatrist to a German

mental home. He wrote a book in which he systematically analysed the scientific and theoretical basis of handwriting psychology, in particular the spontaneity of
writing impulses. The great importance of Meyer was
overshadowed only by the eminence of Dr. Ludwig
Klages, the most important research worker and the
acknowledged high-priest of the German theoretical
school. His achievements and those of Michon together form the real basis of graphology.

Klages, who later moved to Switzerland, wrote many
books on problems of philosophy and the psychology
of expression. He was the first to create a complete and
systematic theory of graphology. It was he who first
saw in it the expression of human personality as a whole,
and fitted it into its place with the other doctrines of
human expression and characterology. He brought the
basic elements of handwriting, which are discussed in
Chapter III, into a system clearly defining the various
meanings of every single handwriting trend, according
to a general law of polarity (that is, the same trend can
denote one quality in one handwriting and the converse
of the same quality in another). Klages based his researches on a conception of writing as a conflict between
natural impulses and rhythms on the one hand, and
mental discipline on the other. He worked out a new
system of analysis determined by a general standard of
handwriting. For him the standard of writing is high
when the writer succeeds in reconciling his genuine
personal rhythm with the requirements of disciplined
writing; the standard is lower by the degree to which he
fails to achieve this reconciliation. By analysing the
changeable and unchangeable elements in handwriting,
he found a way to reveal both intentional and uninten-
tional disguise. But in spite of his great merits, Klages'
system also had deficiencies. In the first place, he over-
emphasized his personality conception; his somewhat

rigid system of compressing human nature into
standards of value based on his ideals of personality does
not allow for the relativity of all tendencies in human
character. He is opposed to the idea that potential
faculties of the same human being can develop in
opposite directions and that the positive and negative
aspects of the same writing tendency can consist in the
same person. This point will be elaborated in the chapter
which deals with analysis.

Secondly, Klages' intellectualism, and his tendency
to supercilious condescension in appreciating the
achievements of the French empirical school, prevented
graphology from developing discoveries by experience
and practical achievement, and inclined it to a more
sterile study of characterological theory. Thirdly, his
slight knowledge of the peculiarities of national characters and handwritings confined his practical achievements to the zone of specifically German text-book
writings and to a specific German conception of character. Fourthly, his somewhat Carlylean conception of
personality resulted in his ignoring the Freudian and
other schools of thought, and so he missed the connection between graphology and the modern psychology of the unconscious.

These last two points—the peculiarities of national
handwriting and the connection between graphology
and the psychology of the unconscious—were developed
by two other men who, basing their ideas on those of
Klages, filled the gap to a certain extent.

The first was Robert Saudek, who came from
Czechoslovakia and finished his main works in England. He was a polyglot who wrote some of his books
in English and some in German. He was especially
concerned with the differences between national characters and national copy-book writing. He made a
special study of English handwriting, in particular the

criterion of speed which is a most important factor. Thus he created a basis for the application of continental research to English handwriting.

The second was Max Pulver, the Swiss, one of the most ingenious of the present generation of graphologists. He partially abandoned Klages' abstract and idealistic conception of personality, and linked graphology with the discoveries of the psychology of the unconscious. As already mentioned in the first chapter, he emphasized the strong symbolic element in handwriting, and especially illuminated the problem of what the writing space symbolizes in the writer's mind.

Apart from these general fields of research, many specialized fields have been investigated by different authors. Let me mention just a few of them.

(1) The identification of handwriting in law-cases has been dealt with by Michon himself, by Dr. Meyer, Busse, the German Schneickert, Weingart and the Austrian Dr. Gross.

(2) The writing of criminals has been extensively studied by Crépieu-Jamin, Langenbruch, Pulver, the Italian psychiatrist, Professor Lombroso, the Austrian Dr. Wieser and many others.

(3) There are excellent studies of children's handwriting by the Frenchman Couilliaux, and a German lady Mina Becker. The German Bahnsen wrote a book to show how graphology can be used for educational purposes.

(4) The expression of the sexual character in handwriting has been investigated, and thrilling discoveries have been made by Georg and Anja Mendelssohn.

(5) Monographs have been written by the Swiss Keller and by the Frenchman Duparchy on the writing of addresses and signatures.

(6) The graphological characteristics of illnesses have been dealt with in many books. A general diagnosis of

all illnesses has been attempted, as for instance in the book by Duparchy, but these attempts have so far proved unsatisfactory. There are, however, many valuable studies of the writing of patients suffering from mental and nervous diseases also of degenerates, made by Lombroso, the German Koster, the Austrian psychiatrist Pick, the Frenchman Dr. Rogues de Fursac and many others.

(7) Handwriting and professional choice have been dealt with by the French collaborating under the direction of Pierre Foix.

Finally a few words on the development of graphology in England. As already mentioned, many great English writers and artists have been attracted by handwriting. A lot of clever remarks on the subject have been made by Scott, Poe, the Brownings, Byron, the painter Gainsborough, Disraeli and others. The first Englishman to deal extensively with the relation between character and handwriting was Stephen Collett, alias Thomas Beverley, who published his book in 1823.

Continental graphology was introduced to England and made popular by Shooling, who translated the main work of Crépieu-Jamin. An English lady Rosa Vaughan also wrote a very useful text-book. The work of the German theoretical school, was brought to England by Robert Saudek, the handwriting expert, novel-writer and polyglot from Prague. Saudek had many pupils of whom one, C. H. Brooks, wrote a text-book based on Saudek's system which was translated into German. In the last years before the 1939-45 war another fairly prominent continental graphologist, H. J. Jacoby, came to England and published some books here, in which he used photographic illustrations in a very clever way to explain the connection between features of handwriting and their pictorial parallels in nature and in human movements.

THE MEANING OF THE BASIC TENDENCIES OF HANDWRITING

Size and width of writing. Form and degree of connection. Regularity and speed. Fullness and pressure. The angle of writing. Right and left tendencies.

I CLOSED the first chapter of general introduction with a warning. When I now come to discuss the special meanings of writing trends, I have to repeat that warning. It should be printed three times at the beginning and end of each chapter in every book on graphology. *No general tendency in handwriting, and no single sign, is by itself adequate to judge a quality in a man's character.* Each tendency has many meanings, and so must be carefully checked with other tendencies and signs which point in the same direction, before a definite statement is made. Human character, and handwriting which is its mirror, are both like a game of cards. The cards are always the same, but the combination in the player's hand, after each shuffle and deal, is always different and unique, so that each game must be examined on its own merits.

Let us now take the list of handwriting terms which appear in Chapter I and analyse them.

SIZE AND WIDTH OF WRITING

Large size writing (see Sample 71) springs from the writer's tendency to need space for himself, small writing from the writer's habit of satisfying himself with the space available to him.

So the tendency of large writing may mean sub-

jectivity, ambition, self-confidence, claims to leadership
and acknowledgment, pathos, enthusiasm, magnanimity
and the general habit or desire to live a rich life on a
large scale; it may also mean the need or habit of ex-
pansive movements, like actors on the stage or orators
at big meetings. But it may also mean lack of objectivity, lack of consideration, of ability to be sub-
ordinate, lack of modesty and tact, carelessness, especially in spending, bossiness and even megalomania.
It may also mean neglect of realities, lack of accuracy,
absent-mindedness and distraction, also a tendency to
be stagey and to be a poseur.

Small handwriting, on the other hand, can mean lack
of self-confidence, inferiority complexes, resignation,
obedience; but also realism, the faculty of observation,
accuracy, reliability, clever husbanding of personal resources, intentional understatement and distaste for
boasting of every kind. It may also mean physical or
mental short-sightedness, sophistication, intolerance,
hypochondria and melancholy.

The size of writing does not give the slightest indication of the height of the writer. There are giants who
write very small and dwarfs who write very large.
Sample 8 shows the writing of a giant, Sample 14b of a
rather under-sized man. The absolute size of handwriting is one of the changeable elements. Therefore
occasional small writing by a person who normally
writes large can only be an adjustment to circumstances
of a technical nature, e.g. lack of space.

So far, I have spoken of the *absolute* size, or more
correctly of the absolute length of writing. There is
also the *relative* length to observe which is, graphologically, also important. What is meant by it is the
relation between the lengths of the short letters (*m, n*
etc.), the so-called middlelengths, and between the
upper and lower parts of the longer letters (*f, g, h*, etc.)

We call the upper part of the longer letters "upper-lengths", the lower part "underlengths". We speak of *relative* large size if the middlelength is above normal (see Sample 31), of *relative* small size if the middle-length is below normal (see Sample 34).

An absolute and relative large size writing (see Samples 41, 36, 118) reveals self-confidence, a high estimate of one's own person and dignity, sometimes condescension, haughtiness and pride.

An absolute large and relative small handwriting (see Sample 77) indicates an exaggerated ambition to be acknowledged which puts a strain on the writer and is difficult to satisfy; it often means a disproportion between the writer's aims and abilities or physical resources.

The middle lengths of letters, like the stem which is the visible part of the tree, symbolize the rational, social, conscious and sentimental part of the human mind; the underlengths, like the root, the unconscious, material, sexual and sub-human aspects; the upper-lengths, like the invisible crown, the spiritual and intellectual spheres. A writing which shows a proper balance between the three lengths indicates an equili-brium of interests between all these different spheres of the human mind. An exaggeration of one length shows the direction in which the writer's interest is exag-gerated at the cost of the others.

Thus an exaggeration of the middlelengths at the expense of the upper and underlengths (see Sample 31) means that rational, social, conscious and sentimental life, with its special satisfaction and dignity, is the focus of the writer's interest. Social self-assurance is always indicated by the relative size of the middlelengths. An exaggeration of the middlelengths always shows that the writer satisfies himself by his position and achievements in the spheres of life just mentioned. If however the extension into the upper and lower lengths is negligible, it is a sign of a phlegmatic and indifferent mind, which has little interest in anything outside its social and rational world (see Samples 47, 121).

You will find this type of handwriting much more often amongst peoples of the Western civilizations, where national ambitions have been fulfilled; whereas the handwriting of restless nations like the Germans shows, even in their copybook writing, an exaggeration of upper and underlengths.

Exaggerated upperlengths, as we have seen (see Sample 48), indicate a tendency towards the intellectual and spiritual spheres, personal culture, many-sided interests, ideals and illusions; but also muddle-headedness, dreaminess, lack of self-discipline, of a solid basis and of a sense of reality.

Exaggerated underlengths (see Samples 49, 50) symbolize realism, the tendency to put everything on a firm, material foundation, the qualities of an organizer; but also lack of illusions, soberness and materialism. The underlengths also reveal the writer's attitude to his unconscious impulses and sexual life. Sexual tendencies in handwriting are a study in themselves; the precision with which all the varieties of sexual inclination and perversities are sometimes mirrored in handwriting is really astonishing. To illustrate this the handwriting of two female homosexuals is given here (Samples 63, 64); you will find some typical modifications (the letter *e* in the word *Erich* and *z* in the German word *ganze*). So far Mendelssohn's book has provided the most comprehensive study of the subject.

Generally speaking, every disproportion in the three lengths, which in normal English handwriting should be the same, indicates a dislocation of the writer's interest and equilibrium. Special attention should be paid when the writer shows a marked disproportion in the same lengths (see Samples 58, 109). This reveals a deficiency in his movements and calls for care, even medical attention.

Let us now study the specific points in a written manuscript where special exaggerations and shortness may occur. These are usually found in the capital letters at the beginning of words. We speak of "Accent on the Start" when these capital letters are above normal in length (see Samples 46, 64). It is a sign of showing off, a call for attention, an exaggeration of the writer's self and importance. An adjustment of capital letters to the size of the others, on the other hand (see Sample 31), shows a tendency to understatements often acquired by education. If the length of the letters gradually shortens (see Sample 29), it means pride or condescension. If capital letters, especially letters with three parts like the capital "M", mount in size, it is a sign of a mixture of outward showing-off with inner subordination to the opinion of others, and to public opinion in general (see Sample 78).

Increasing size at the end of words will generally be found in the handwriting of children. It is the tendency to look up to the world of adults, also the tendency to become more and more frank. If found in the handwriting of adults, it shows that they are still in an infantile, uncomplicated state of mind and merely blurt out what they think (see Sample 54). In cultured and intelligent handwritings, it indicates a tendency to frankness, bald statements and lack of diplomacy.

Diminishing size at the end of words shows maturity, the faculty of making oneself so unobtrusive that there is no opposition on the other person's part. In other words, this means diplomacy (see Sample 5). If the same letters within words are constantly larger than the others (see Sample 61) I have found this shows that the writer attaches some peculiar importance to generally unimportant facts. Such people are usually very touchy and always jealous.

As for the significance of the width of handwriting, broad writing (see Sample 43) originates from an unrestricted movement of the hand in a lateral direction; narrow writing, on the other hand, is a sign of restriction. The basic meaning of broad writing is consequently a lack of restriction in the social sphere. The broad writer wants room for his person; he likes large rooms, wants to travel, to spend lavishly on himself, his food, clothing and hobbies. He mostly thinks in cosmopolitan terms. He indulges in great detail in speaking about himself and often cares little whether his audience is interested or not. He can be self-assured, egotistic, indiscreet, vain and full of pride. He may lack concentration, discipline and real tact. On the other hand he is mostly broadminded, natural and tolerant. His attitude to others is normally one of routine frankness and friendliness. He likes to oblige and to extend invitations, but is also usually prepared to take advantage of others. He is certainly a poor candidate for a marriage which is not on a generous social scale, or for any condition in which people have to live and work closely together and consider each other's convenience.

The narrow writer (see Sample 31) is inhibited and full of restrictions. He shows discipline and concentration; he is economical, often even mean and distrustful. He may be narrow-minded and intolerant. If narrow writing is a feature of the capital letters at the beginning of words (see Sample 39), it indicates shyness. Broad and large capital letters on the other hand (see Sample 122) especially if there is a dividing stroke between the two parts of the letter, as sometimes in the capital H in Hitler's signature, for example, are indicative of a vulgar form of self-conceit and even arrogance and impertinence.

FORM AND DEGREE OF CONNECTION

The copy-book form of connection (see Sample 65) indicates, in a quick and personal writing, that the writer attaches value to keeping to conventions and has a talent for doing so. In slow and impersonal copy-book writing (see Sample 42) it means lack of genuineness and originality; sometimes, as for instance in the case of the handwriting of some criminals, it means disguise, in the form of a conventional mask.

Angular connection (see Sample 31) shows that the writer does not mind the effort imposed on him by this form of connection and that he prefers firmness to compromise. Angular writers have mostly a capacity for persistence, or at least passive resistance, and are in this or some other respect hard and uncompromising. This imposes restrictions on them, makes them often resentful and revengeful, even sulky and cruel. As workers they will undertake difficult tasks, as they do not mind overcoming difficulties. Generally they are more reliable than gracious.

Of the rounded forms of connection the *garland* (see Sample 35) is a sign of amiability, open friendliness, kindness, softness of nature, sometimes merely of routine thoughtlessness and weakness.

The *arcade* (see Sample 66) originating from a covering, protective gesture, symbolizes diplomatic courtesy, a polite screening of one's own thoughts, also impenetrability, a calm and calculating attitude, sometimes moral and friendly. It also may mean lying and hypocrisy.

Wavy lines (see Sample 56) resembling the movement of a snake or the surface of the sea, represent in intelligent and energetic handwriting the highest degree of diplomacy (see Sample 79) (Churchill a wavy-line writer), the faculty of changing front. It can also in less strongly individual handwritings indicate a tendency to avoid all decisions, and the lack of firm character (see Sample 56).

If the letters of a word and their connections degenerate into a single thread, especially inside words (see Sample 55) which makes the words partly illegible, it shows a caprice, lack of conviction and firm purpose, and is in the main a sign of hysteria. Both wavy line and thread connection indicate, on the other hand, a high degree of changeability and suggestibility.

The covering stroke (see Samples 38, 65) which is found in arcade, garland and angular connection, is a sign of the greatest restriction. The writer holds onto the railings as long as possible before he takes the next step. He is distrustful to the utmost degree, hides his plans and intentions and puts feelers out like a snail from its shell. He prefers to remain anonymously in the background until he feels safe to come out in the open. It is a sign of an exaggerated and chronic sense of personal security, the symbol of the tactician, the man with a mask, behind which lies physical disability or bitter experience or simply a fear of open fight.

The degree of connection is an important element and a very difficult thing to change. A connected handwriting (see Sample 38) shows that when putting the image of a word on paper the writer is not deflected by other ideas, that his thoughts are proceeding in logical and methodical sequence, and that he is able to adjust himself (which does not necessarily mean that he wants to). If connection is overdone, especially if a whole sentence is connected (see Sample 57), it shows an excessive desire to look for relationships which are remote, sophistication to an absurd degree. On the Continent such handwritings are regarded as typical of inventors of chess and bridge problems and psychoanalysts. In Great Britain, country of cross-word puzzles, weekly competitions, quizzes and Brains Trusts, they are quite frequent too. The exaggeration of connection is sometimes also a sign of lack of power of distinction and sense of the *nuances* of life; such people want to force things which do not belong together into a system; with them it is a question of adjustment by force and logic to the point of lunacy.

Disconnected writing (see Sample 34) shows that the writer has many different ideas which influence him so much that he has to interrupt the course of his thoughts. You will find it in the writing of many people of unusual imagination and intuitive genius, but also in the writing of the illogical and the abrupt-minded, who lack concentration and method and who miss the main point through too much attention to details. If you find *both* frequent and large intervals inside words (see Samples 74, 76) this is a sign of serious overstrain of the mind, likely to result in sporadic black-outs and loss of memory. A man who writes like that has great difficulty in mastering all the quick-changing and distracting ideas, and if he is not cared for in time it may lead to complete mental breakdown and loss of memory. A break of letters into parts (see Sample 81) is also a sign of unsoundness. There is no agreement up to now amongst graphologists as to the meaning of this, but all of them would say that it is the sign of a person who is very difficult to deal with. An abrupt change from very connected to very disconnected handwriting indicates a tendency to mental disease.

Certain breaks in vertical up and down strokes have organic roots and may come from an organic shock this is usually the case with people suffering from heart trouble.

The faculty of connecting the dot over the "i", accents and the "t" cross with following or preceding letters (see Samples 67, 70) shows an outstanding faculty for logical combination and usually an ability for scientific research.

REGULAR writing (see Sample 45) is a sign of a regular mind. If regularity is simply of the copy-book style, it is an indication of lack of vitality, personality and imagination; otherwise it shows will-power, a balanced mind and sense of harmony. It also shows singularity of purpose, lack of excitability, lack of capacity to change and sometimes pedantry and monotony.

Irregular writing (see Sample 80) shows many-sided interests, multiple and changing purposes, excitability, capacity to change, but also nervousness, changing moods, lack of steadiness and tidiness.

If an irregular handwriting is rhythmic (see Sample 79) it indicates calmness and equilibrium, but sometimes also indifference. Unrhythmic handwriting is a sign of a high degree of emotionality, a passionate character, abrupt changes of temper and an instability of the sympathetic nervous system (see Sample 80).

SPEED

The SPEED of handwriting is interesting from many points of view. One has to keep in mind that writing is a routine which is learnt by memorizing visually the images of letters and letter groups (words) and then tracing them on paper. The speed at which this routine is exercised depends on the mastery of these preconditions. The child, the unintelligent and unskilled writer, the heavy manual worker (see Sample 54) the ill and the weak will all be handicapped in remembering the images of words or in working out the writing. Concentration on the mere process of tracing the letters will be one of the reasons for slow writing. Thus it may indicate a low standard of learning, debility of memory or intelligence, or deficiencies of normal skill caused by ill-health or a heavy hand. Whether a writer who has mastered handwriting writes quickly or slowly depends in the first instance on whether he is primarily concerned with the contents of his writing only, or whether he is also bearing in mind how his writing will look. Quick writing (see Sample 1) is a sign of a person who is spontaneous, objective and pertinent. Slow writing (see Sample 46) is calculated writing. Quick writing indicates a quick grasp of things, intelligence and spontaneity of mind as well as of emotion, topical enthusiasm; also neglect of details and hastiness. Slow writing—in so far as it does not originate in a slow mind or a slow hand—is calculated, unspontaneous writing. The writer is "writing-conscious". It is not only the "what" but also the "how" that he is always aware of. He is concerned not only with the point he is making, but also the style in which he makes it. This will be the case with everybody who attaches value to personal style of an aesthetic nature (see Sample 26), who paints his writing for the sake of painting. Thus painters and artistic minds, indulging in the working out of aesthetic details and ornaments, will write slowly. So will the man who calculates to give by his writing the impression of a certain style of living, e.g. the poseur, the snobbish dandy and the adventurous swindler (see Sample 61).

Slow writing will also be the writing of a man who calculates the effect of every manifestation and expression of himself; for instance the thorough person who attends to every detail, also the pedant. Slowness is also a sign of emotional slowness i.e. phlegm, and of mental slowness, laziness.

Among the calculated writings, disguised writings have a special place. The man who by his handwriting wants to appear a different character to what he really

is, is always "writing conscious" and writes slowly.
People who want to change their handwriting deliberately also have to write slowly; for instance, the anonymous letter writer or the criminal who does not want to be recognized by his handwriting. It is difficult for the most skilled writer, even if he is a graphologist and even by writing slowly, to change the basic elements in his writing, especially relative length, degree of connection, etc. In quick writing change of this nature is virtually impossible.

Finally, the forger who copies another person's handwriting has to do it slowly. Often the only sign by which the forgery can be detected is found in comparing the reproduction with the quickly written original. The speed of handwriting therefore becomes the decisive factor in ascertaining the genuineness and spontaneity of all the other signs of handwriting; it is the most important branch of study for the expert graphologist, who has to deal in court with disguised or forged handwriting. As spontaneity and a tendency to be calculating are both present in most human minds you will find signs both of speed and of slowness in most handwritings.

FULLNESS, LEANNESS AND DEGREE OF PRESSURE

Full writing (see Sample 41) is achieved neither by the length nor width of the letters, but by their forms, by arcs, slopes and circles, covering more space than lean writing of the same length and width; just as the man with imagination ranges over larger fields of life than a man of the same intellectual standard without imagination. Full writing means imagination, vision and a creative mind. But it can also indicate a tendency to wander from the point, to indulge in fancy.

Lean writing, on the other hand (see Sample 28), may

disclose a faculty for abstract thinking, for sticking to essentials, but also lack of imagination and soberness.

PRESSURE, which played an important part in early graphological research, has lost some of its significance owing to the change from the quill pen to the fountain pen which makes the production of lines varying widely in thickness more difficult for the writer. In spite of that, even with the fountain-pen the application of strong and weak pressure is still possible. Why does one man use stronger pressure in writing than another? It may simply originate from a strong vitality and driving force which delights in expressing itself. It may come from a heavy hand. It can also spring from a feeling that pressure and force are necessary to overcome outer or inner resistance, "from a heavy hand or a heavy mind" as Klages puts it.

Thus strong pressure (see Sample 9) can mean energy and vitality enjoying its own vigour. It can also mean that the writer is not used to writing and needs the application of force in order to do it. It may mean, alternatively, that the writer's hand is heavy because of his calling, e.g. a blacksmith, or because of some recreation such as that of a sportsman used to applying strong muscular pressure. Finally, it can indicate that a person is so full of repressions, fears, pessimism or melancholy, that he needs to make a heavy effort to overcome it, or that he is so brutal that he believes only in force. In judging pressure, it will be necessary in any case to examine the kind of pen with which the manuscript was written and whether there were any special technical difficulties present which made the use of heavy pressure necessary in that particular instance.

Slight pressure (see Sample 35) shows that the writer is either clever and skilled enough to write with the minimum of energy, or that he dislikes applying any unnecessary energy or force, or that he is too weak to do so. Thus soft pressure writing is either the writing of the skilled person who economizes his own powers or of the soft-hearted individual who hates force and brutality, or of the weakling.

Pasty writing (see Samples 31, 38, 40), gives the observer the impression of intense shading and colourfulness. It has a sensual rather than a spiritual effect and it does symbolize sensuality, a liking for the sensual pleasures of life, for colours and brightness, for nature and art, for food and drink, for kissing and love-making. All sensual types of human personalities, from the artist to the *gourmand*, from the master of the art of living to the man who is driven to excesses by his impulses, will be found amongst the pasty writers.

The opposite of pasty handwriting is thin handwriting (see Sample 76). Such writers are not sensitive to the refinements of life, the *nuances*, the happy little banalities, but are brainy, critical, dependent on principles and morals, even ascetic, but also uncreative, pedantic, vindictive, malicious, boring, unable to enjoy life.

It has been said before that the question of pressure and shading depends more than any other on technicalities, i.e. the kind of pen, paper and ink which is used. But here it should be added that the choice of these materials, in so far as there is a choice, is largely a matter of personal taste. This is particularly true of the kind of ink used. Only a banal and unimaginative person will constantly use a watery, washy-looking blue ink. Only a pedant or a know-all, or a member of one of the pedantic or "know-all" professions, a schoolmaster, accountant or a lawyer, will constantly enjoy the use of red ink. Dark violet ink, especially when used on coloured writing paper, indicates a keenness to be fashionable. A preference for green ink shows a liking to be apart and distinguished. The alternative use of different coloured inks, especially in order to underline words, is a reliable indication that the writer is a fool of some kind.

THE ANGLES OF WRITING : RIGHT AND LEFT TENDENCIES

If a man stands upright, he gives the impression of being an independent individual. If he leans forward he seems to be longing for other people and to depend on them. If he leans backwards, one has the feeling that he is afraid of other people and wants to be separate from them, but that like the man who leans forward, and unlike the man who stands upright, he is very conscious of the existence of others. These three positions will serve to represent the angles of writing.

Upright writing (see Sample 12) means independence. Writing slanting to the right (see Sample 11) means extraversion. Writing slanting backwards (see Sample 58) means introversion and isolation.

The human being who writes upright will be the less dependent on outside influences which he will meet in a cool, calm even phlegmatic manner. The writer who slants to the right will be social and socially excitable and the more pronounced the slant to the right is, the more passionately he will long for the regard of others, for success or recognition in the social sphere. Such writers will be capable of strong sentiments of love and hate, strong passions, and also of self-sacrifice. Sentimentality, enthusiasm, social activity, altruism, but also restlessness, excitable temperament, lack of discipline and common sense, and obtrusiveness are the main characteristics of writers who slant to the right.

A writer who slants backwards to the left lives in an inner state of isolation; but he is aware of living in a world which compels him to take note of it. Writing which slants backwards is always a sign of an artificial approach to others, of a kind of routine which hides the writer's introverted mind. People of this kind are always a little forced, affected and elusive. One can never really get hold of them. As the left side of the page means mother, past, childhood and the parents' house, people whose writing slants to the left will mostly look backwards and will not be able to get rid of memories of childhood and of the early years of life. The backward slanting writer is a person who hides his secret paradise from the eyes of his fellow men. All the different types of split personality, egocentric narcissists and men with a Freudian Oedipus complex are indicated by the backward slant.

The backward slant is not learnt in any copy-book form. The teaching of upright writing or writing sloping to the right varies according to the country and to the period. These variations are also always strongly indicative of the general spirit and mood of a nation and the temper and spirit of the times (*Zeitgeist*). In the rationalistic period of early Humanism, people wrote upright. In the sentimental and enthusiastic era of Werther and Byron slanted writing became the fashion and remained in fashion until fifty years ago. Since then with the appearance of the ideal of common sense and cool reason, of the calm and independent gentleman, upright writing became once again the copy-book form in Great Britain, whereas the passionate and restless Germans still went on slanting to the right.

In judging handwriting, therefore, it is always necessary to ascertain the age and nationality of the writer in order to find out what copy-book form he has learnt at school. The variation from this copy-book style is from the point of view of graphology very significant.

It remains for us to consider an individual writing in which slanting to the right alternates with slanting backwards and upright writing (see Samples 92, 95, 99).

This is indicative of an inner conflict between heart and brain, sentimental and reasonable tendencies, altruistic, actual and egotistical motives.

Quite apart from the actual slanting of writing to the left or to the right, there are other discernible tendencies in handwriting to the left and to the right. The extension of starting strokes, crossing strokes or end strokes, or the exaggeration of slopes to the right or to the left (see Sample 62) are the most frequent ones. The exaggeration to the right is always a sign of giving, also of running to others, the tendency to the left, (see Samples 46, 48, 61, 16, 17) of retiring, of collecting and of bringing home. The altruist as well as the busybody, the magnanimous donor as well as the restless and the impressionable person will show tendencies to the right. The man of common sense, the collector and the contemplative person as well as the greedy, the envious, the egotistical, will be amongst the left tendency writers. The profit motive too is always indicated by a tendency to the left.

An exaggerated tendency to the left can also be shown by writing addresses and signatures on the left hand side of the page. As the signature is in the writer's mind the most pronounced symbol of his own personality, the placing of a signature on the extreme left indicates a high degree of inner isolation, of retreat from the human world to the very origin, of desire to re-enter the mother's body—to leave the world altogether. If it is combined with backward slanting writing, small writing and weak pressure, you can, with a high degree of certainty, assume strong suicide tendencies. Another sign of suicide tendencies is the crossing through of the writer's own name, the so-called "stroke through the ego" in the signature.

This finishes, for the limited purposes of this book, the chapter about the basic tendencies of handwriting.

In the presentation of it I have closely followed the Central European school which culminated in the systems of Pulver and Klages, to which Jacoby and Saudek also belong. This school, contrary to the French school led by Crépieu-Jamin, tries to cover the main features by a few general terms and by giving the different possibilities and meanings of the same feature, to keep to as few headings as possible. Crépieu-Jamin does the opposite by developing a rich nomenclature of 165 graphological trends. His follower de Rougemont, while asserting the necessity of keeping to essentials and not embarrassing the student with too many terms, still retains 110 of them, grouped into forty-one groups.

While appreciating the immense amount of empirical discovery which is revealed in this wealth of annotation, and the necessity of dealing with it all in any more advanced study, I feel that in an introduction like this an economic use of terminology is more practical and less embarrassing for the reader and student, especially the beginner.

It is, however, interesting that the last trends in French graphology, as shown in the books of Madame Saint-Morand, restrict this huge terminology and tend to reduce the general layout and elaboration of handwriting to four degrees of simplification and complication and the basic elements to eight groups (arrangement, extension, pressure, form of connection, speed, degree of connection, angle of writing, direction).

CHAPTER IV

GENERAL LAYOUT AND ELABORATION OF HANDWRITING

*Arrangement, Margins, Spacing, Lines, Simplification
and Complication, Degree of Attention.*

WHEN a trained gardener surveys the ground on which he is to lay out a garden, he will formulate a plan quickly in his mind—where to plant the tree and flowers, where to leave the ground unplanted and how to arrange and organize the whole. Another man may start haphazardly and continue to plant, without a plan, and his garden will look badly arranged and unorganized.

When a man has to fill an empty sheet of paper with his handwriting he is in a similar position. If he has a good idea how to dispose of the space economically, a sense for organization, proportion and clever distribution, he will place his writing on the paper so as to give the impression that in the moment of starting to write he has an immediate conception of how to do it (see Sample 69). The writing of another person may give just the opposite effect (see Samples 85, 105). Thus a well arranged general layout will indicate to you intelligent disposition of time and space, a good faculty of conception and distribution and organizing insight. In addition, if the writing is quick it is a sign of quick grasp of situations and the faculty of making decisions in time. On the other hand, it may indicate a tendency to put brain and organization before natural instincts and spontaneous impulses, and if it is overdone it may mean intellectual pride and snobbery.

A badly arranged general layout may indicate the contrary: lack of appreciation of time and space, lack of economy in both, lack of the faculty of arrangement and organization, a poor sense of time-table, constant muddle, lack of the ability to make decisions in time. On the other hand, it may mean genuineness, a fertile and spontaneous mind which does not work by plan and preparation but starts from scratch.

As to the margins on the left and right hand side of the line, a constant distance at the beginning of the line from the left hand edge of the sheet (see Sample 82) indicates a constancy in behaviour which is a sign of good manners and at least external tact. It is also a sign of consistency in work. If this distance from the left hand edge becomes larger as the page of writing progresses (see Sample 117), it means a tendency to fatigue as work progresses and to let oneself go after a certain time. The opposite development is indicated if the distance becomes smaller (see Sample 110).

If the beginning of the line is very close to the margin (see Sample 83) it shows a tendency to, or a necessity for, economy of time and money, and in extreme cases, stinginess. If the distance becomes greater later on in the page it shows an intention to economize, an intention which is later partly dropped in practice.

Large distances between the left edge and the start of the lines (see Sample 82) show that the writer is used to living on a lavish scale, or wants to do so, and does not care for saving or economizing. If the distances get smaller (see Sample 110) it indicates that his lavishness was rather in the nature of mere showing off and that he is really keen on saving his pennies.

The behaviour of the writer at the end of the line is also of some relevance. If he can always end the line with a normal complete word, without having to split a word onto the next line or compress the writing of the last word, it shows that the writer has a quick and clear comprehension, power of surveying and the faculty of decision (see Sample 63). If he leaves too much space at the end of the line (see Sample 87) it shows careless-ness, neglect and a spendthrift nature. If he has a tendency to leave no space (see Sample 90) either by extending endstrokes right to the end of the line, or even by inserting strokes to fill the empty space, it shows extreme distrustfulness and unconscious fear that the empty space may be filled by somebody else.

The behaviour at the end of pages and the end of letters is also very interesting. A man who likes to post-pone decisions always hesitates to turn over the page until it is really unavoidable. Thus if a person who has not compressed words and lines till the end of the page then starts narrow writing and fills up the page to the very end, he is certainly a person who dislikes decisions and does not make them until he has no other choice.

If at the end of letters a man starts writing across in the margin and empty spaces until there is no more room, it may, in a lesser degree, indicate the same tendencies, lack of decision or over-economy. But the most important meaning is that the writer does not know when to finish and make a clean break. He is one of those persons who go on talking things over when the matter is already closed, stays loitering behind in the doorway when the other guests have departed and in this way wastes his and other people's time.

In judging the general outlay, it is always useful to have more than one manuscript of the writer, as he may have had to compress and fit his writing into too narrow a space like a small card owing to paper shortage, etc. and therefore to adjust his writing in a special case to unusual technical circumstances.

As to spacing, the distance between letters inside words has already been discussed. What we are concerned with here is the distance between words and lines. Clear spacing between words (see Sample 27) means clearmindedness, intellectual culture and skill, braininess, discerning and critical faculties. It is also a sign of a sense of distance and a scale of values and categories. In extreme cases (see Sample 93) it means intellectual pride and snobbery, isolation which may lead to the melancholy of the isolated mind. In cases where people, who hitherto have not done so, suddenly start to put large intervals between words, it shows, according to Klages, a desperate effort to maintain clear and distinct thought, which is often followed by a mental breakdown. Narrow spacing between words (see Sample 85) means lack of sense of distance, and distinction, lack of tact, obtrusiveness, lack of clear-mindedness, but on the other hand warmth and spontaneity.

The connection of many words and whole sentences (see Sample 57) without spacing, as already mentioned, is a sign of an uncritical sense of logic and adjustment which seeks to put things together which should be kept separate and even to force a link.

Irregular spacing (see Sample 102), shows varying degrees of clearmindedness and sense of distance.

Writing in which the lines are kept clear and do not run into each other, especially in the case of large hand-writing, is a sign of a clever mind and intellectual skill. The interweaving of lines and the mixing up of the underlengths of the upper line with upperlengths, or even middlelengths of the following line (see Sample 43) is a sign of muddleheadedness and lack of the power to survey, lack of critical sense and intellectual skill and clear expression in favour of spontaneity and sometimes of ingenuity. In cases of handwriting which is highly individualistic, it is, as Saudek has shown in the case of the writings of Kant and Beethoven, a sign of great men so much occupied with their own ideas that they care little whether others can follow them or not.

Mounting lines (see Sample 30) are a sign of optimism, enthusiasm, fighting spirit and ambition. In extreme cases they may indicate a kind of frenzy or mania.

Descending lines (see Sample 33) indicate pessimism, depression, criticism, also ill-health, tiredness and weakness, lack of muscular and nervous energy, either in the hand or in the whole organism. Combined with dirty, pasty and neglected writing, it indicates a bad digestion.

A mounting signature is a sign of professional ambition (see Sample 37).

A line which first goes up and then descends like an arc (see Sample 60) is characteristic of people who are quickly enthusiastic but who lack persistence. These are the people who are always starting something new but get tired of the project before it is finished and bears fruit. They do not like to stick to any one job and are always getting interested in something different and looking for a change.

In contrast to this is the line of writing which descends first but then rises again like an inverted arc (see Sample 35). This is the writing of a person who through hard circumstances or physical weakness gets tired but has the mental energy to stick it out, to regain strength and to work up and use the faculties to the fullest in the end.

Those whose lines of writing first rise and then descend are brilliant starters, those whose lines first descend and then rise are reliable finishers.

If the line falls first and then rises more than once in a line (see Sample 40) we are dealing with a person who has to fight on against continuous discouragement but who wins through in the end by continuous mental effort. The handwriting of the famous writer Thomas Mann provides a good example of this.

The general evolution of a man's handwriting away from the copy-book form can move either in the direction of complication, amplification and floridity, or in the direction of simplification, even to the neglecting of whole parts of letters.

The choice between these two directions of general elaboration is in the first instance a matter of personal taste.

The writer who complicates and makes additions to the copy-book form of letters, or at any rate enlarges parts of letters (see Samples 48, 61, 73), dislikes the simple matter-of-fact approach to what is useful and essential; he needs the more ornamental and baroque style for his personal satisfaction. Simplification moves in the direction of the essential and the topical complication in the direction of the impressive and the decorative.

Thus a tastefully amplified handwriting (Sample 41) discloses a taste for decorative forms and presentation, for effects and arrangement—a creative æstheticism, but also a certain fussiness. An overdose of florid complication which sometimes overshadows the basic feature of the letters and makes them hardly readable can be either a sign of bad and vulgar taste, vanity, boastfulness, posing, or a tendency to be a busybody, fussiness, affection, pomposity, cumbersome lack of realism, and complexes of different kinds always with a view to impressing somebody. (Samples 37, 122.)

The clever and tasteful, simplified and yet readable handwriting (see Samples 67, 79) means intellectual discipline, keeping to essentials, abhorrence of loud effects, sublimation, realism, but also soberness, lack of sense of beauty and of appreciation of anything which does not serve a purpose. It means also the attaching of little or no importance to presentation.

Neglected handwriting (see Sample 44) indicates

untidiness in dress, in the home and in personal habits. If it is so neglected that it is difficult to read it indicates a tendency to be ambiguous, to cover up, to be obscure.

The degree of attention paid to various phases of the writing is also an important aspect of the general layout. If a writer starts in a regular and rhythmic way and in the course of the script becomes irregular and non-rhythmic, if at the beginning his handwriting is clear and legible and later becomes neglected and illegible, it is a sign that he lacks staying power. If he starts slowly and becomes quicker, or vice-versa, it also gives an indication of his method of working. If his lines are at first straight and then descend, one sees that the writer has become tired in the course of doing the work.

Again, if one of the basic elements, such as big and small writing, the angle of writing etc., changes towards the end, when the writing becomes quicker, you can be sure that the latter is the real tendency of the writer and that his behaviour at the start was only calculated to hide his true character (see Sample 46).

There are other points calling for special attention. These are the beginnings and ends of words. Inside a word, the writer has less freedom to form the letters according to his personal liking, but at the start and at the end the pen makes a break, and the writer can form and extend his strokes more freely. We have already dealt with the size and width of capital letters, about words missing or descending or even degenerating at the end, about end-strokes extending to the right or to the left. There remain a few more things to add.

If the writer uses a starting stroke (see Sample 36), it shows that he needs some inner preparation to start. If these strokes are extended far beyond the normal line (see Samples 89, 103) the person has a busy nature, always on the move, and does many superfluous things before coming to the real issue. These traits are in the main connected with a fighting spirit which often even gets quarrelsome and litigious, combative and obstinate.

The writer who starts immediately and even leaves out the beginning stroke of the copybook (see Samples 27, 38) shows quick comprehension and the faculty of grasping immediately the heart of a matter. It is often a sign of a tendency to do nothing more than what is barely necessary, neglecting extras, even pleasant extras, and it can be the sign of an inclination to melancholy.

The writer who starts with an arc (see Samples, 112, 113) likes to hear the sound of his own voice and has a tendency to emphasize. If the arc starts to the right of the letter and goes back to the left (see Sample 115) it indicates the actor, either professional or in private life.

The writer who starts with a point on which his pen rests in delight for a while (see Samples 96, 104, 116) shows satisfaction in material achievements and possessions.

An end-stroke going back to the left and ending in a point (see Samples 86, 114) indicates purposeful flattery.

If the end-stroke forms a garland and then rises up as though to heaven (see Sample 105) it is the sign of a religious nature.

If the writer breaks up his words with the downstroke and omits the extending stroke to the right which copybook form prescribes (see Sample 51) it means a tendency to abrupt breaking off of social relations, friendships and contacts and in specific cases also a tendency to save money.

Constant amendments especially of the upper parts of letters (see Samples 59, 100) are a sign of a neurotic type of excessive sensitivity and of hypochondria.

Big curved starting strokes (see Samples 61, 111) are a sign of greed.

An endstroke which is curved like a coxcomb (see Samples 91, 95) means hot temper.

In this presentation of layout and elaboration I again followed the system and terminology of the German School and Klages; but the next chapter is based on the splendid achievements of the French school of Michon, Crépieu-Jamin and the empiricists in France and other countries, in particular Rudolphine Poppée.

CHAPTER V

T CROSSING, DOTS ON THE I AND PUNCTUATION

YOU will remember the different crossings of the T shown in Chapter I. When the T is crossed, the writer interrupts his writing. The T cross normally has no connection either with the preceding or the following letter. So the writer has complete liberty to move his pen in whatever direction he wishes. This emancipates him completely from the T cross of the copybook form and allows him to make it according to his personal taste. Thus, when the writer consistently forms his T cross in the same manner, it is an independent graphological sign of great importance. Some types of Ts are self-explanatory.

If someone writes Ts like notes and musical keys (see Samples 25, 60), he is certainly musical.

If a person omits the whole letter and only makes the cross (see Sample 26) it can have no other meaning than that he attaches great importance to things which are only of secondary importance to other people and omits, overlooks or pretends to ignore what to others seems to be the principal thing.

If the T cross is full of hooks (see Sample 10) it can be readily assumed that the writer is difficult, obstinate and pig-headed.

If the writer is capable of writing the T upside down (see Sample 22), it can be taken that he will not object to treating facts in the same way.

If the cross turns backward and overhead (see Sample 23) like a forearm bent protectively over a person's head, you will yourself have imagined that the writer is the kind of person who protects his independence in a fanatical and pugnacious fashion, sometimes when it is not in any way threatened.

That a neat connection of the T cross with the following letter (see Sample 21) is the sign of a clever mind that grasps things quickly, full of ability for scientific combination and research, will also be easily understood.

The explanation of other types of T cross is not so obvious. The little series of sketches which follow associate the particular of the T cross with a symbol, a gesture or an image which lies behind it. This will make the meaning clearer to you. It will also give you a more substantial impression of the pictorial, the ideographic and the symbolic element in writing about which you will learn more in the next chapter.

Now let us look at the various T crosses one by one. Mrs. Elias's amusing sketches on the next few pages help to make their meanings clear at a glance.

There are yet other meanings of the T crosses. Short ones (see Sample 19) mean concentration; long thin ones (see Sample 6) impulsiveness but lack of stamina; regular ones (see Sample 3) even application of energy; irregular ones (see Sample 40) a changing degree of application of it.

As with the T cross, the dot over the *i* has no connection with the preceding or following letter, and so if always written in the same manner is a definite and important graphological sign. So is the forming of punctuation, and in some foreign languages the accents and marks over vocal sounds, which however need not be considered here.

Correct placing of the dot over the *i* (see Sample 52) is a sign of accuracy. For some professions such as surgeons, dentists and fine mechanics, accurate work is so essential that the dotting of the *i* is an important

1

Desire to protect, authority, a fatherly spirit.

2

Quick thinking, enterprise, thoughts running ahead of action. haste.

3

Obedience, a tendency to be subservient.

4

Ego-centricity.

5

A longing to be at the top, bossiness, ambition.

6

Mental gymnastics. The man who solves cross-word puzzles or chess problems in his lunch hour frequently writes like that.

7

Vanity, also sometimes prejudice. In addition it can mean automatic and superficial friendliness.

8

Grabbing, pocketing, greed for money and material goods, the profit-motive and egotism.

9

Pugnacity, an ambitious but quarrelsome and litigious tendency.

10

Coercion, despotism, blackmail, lack of.tolerance, or at any rate fanatical objection to any interference in the writer's affairs.

11

Demonstrative happiness, unconcealed satisfaction about the achievements of oneself and one's family.

12

(**No cross at all and rounded at the bottom.**) Physical weakness **and sometimes** in consequence laziness and indifference.

The man in the sky, high flying ideas and dreams, also preoccupation with matters aerial. Einstein writes like that; and see Sample 1, which is taken from the writing of a former British Air Minister.

A sense of fun.

Discouragement of activity in others, sulkiness, spiteful **and** envious criticism, non-co-operation.

16

The hand on the brake. It is a sign of caution, restraint, meditation, delaying tactics. Earl Baldwin wrote like that.

17

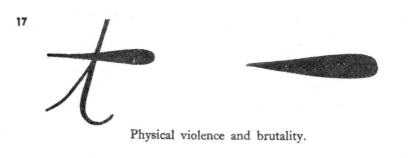

Physical violence and brutality.

18

Mental cruelty and aggressiveness, wounding criticism and malice.

19

The knot, a sign of toughness and thoroughness.

indication whether a man qualifies for one of these vocations. It is also a criterion of a sense for detailed work.

If the dot of the *i* is close to the top of the letter (see Samples 104, 107) it indicates subservience; if it is in addition heavy (see Sample 74) it is a sign of a deeply depressed mind.

High-flying dots over the *i* (see Sample 48) point to high flying ideals as well as to lack of accuracy.

In cube form (see Samples 1, 74) they indicate vitality, even brutality.

Dots to the right of the *i* (see Sample 2) indicate enterprise and quick running thoughts, to the left (see Sample 96) they are a sign of hesitating caution.

If connected with the next letter or with the T cross (see Sample 70) they disclose good ability for combination and scientific research.

If the dot is in the form of a small open arc (see Sample 107) it is a sign of sincerity, kindness and sometimes of religious feeling.

An inverted rolling arc or a horizontal stroke (see Sample 106) symbolizes covering up, diplomacy and also lying.

If it has the shape of a little triangle or an open arc facing the right (see Samples 52, 59, 84) the so-called "watching eye", it is one of the most important indications of very highly developed faculty of observation.

If in comma form, sharpening at the bottom (see Sample 63) it indicates a critical intellect.

As for punctuation, the same principles appropriately adjusted apply to the shapes of full-stops and commas. The omission of all punctuation indicates carelessness and negligence and lack of consideration, as the excessive use of punctuation, of hyphens, full-stops and underlinings indicates insistence, a rather snobbish, vain, affected and foolish emphasis on the writer's own point of view.

Commas that are too long (see Sample 85) mean an over-emphasis of principles.

The putting of a full stop, or even a stop and a hyphen after the signature of a person is a sign of pedantry, caution, distrust, also of marked conventionality.

If the writing is often interrupted by little sketches replacing words by drawings of hearts, animals, etc., it springs usually from the mind of an imbecile or a lunatic.

A vertical crossing of letters on the inside slopes or strokes prescribed by the copybook is always found to be a sign of low cunning, deceit and petty snobbery. If this stroke does not replace another one but is merely inserted as an ornamental addition it has not only the same meaning as before but discloses in addition a vulgar taste and a high degree of impudence. This sign used in both ways is very frequently found in Hitler's handwriting.

CHAPTER VI

SIGNS, MOVEMENTS, GESTURES, SYMBOLS

HAVING examined the significance of general lay-out, basic elements, and various other signs like the T cross, and having partly explained some of the reasons why special meanings are attached to the particular elements, we are still faced—as we were in Chapter One—with the theoretical question whether it is possible to offer a general explanation of the causal link between the individual character and the individual handwriting.

In the early days of graphology there was little enquiry into reasons. The signs were discovered by experience and simply accepted. Even to-day many signs exist which in practice prove reliable, though no explanation of them can be found as for other handwriting signs. It is more or less generally accepted that the forming of the small letter *r* with the first part much higher than the second means curiosity; but none of the usual explanations, as found for other elements, will explain this fact. We have simply to refute or accept it by our own experience. There may, however, be a possible explanation for that. An *r* formed in this way divides the letter into two watching eyes open to the right, which are a sign of observation. The curious man is always a keen observer.

Other signs can be explained in a simple way by the biological and physical reasons for the movement. That a person of high vitality and a heavy hand uses greater pressure than a person of low vitality is self-explanatory on a physical basis. That quick movement produces

75

quicker writing than slow movement, that disciplined and inhibited movements produce a more disciplined and inhibited writing than free movements can also be readily understood. Other tendencies and signs also spring obviously to mind from the corresponding mental qualities, habits and gifts of the writer. That a man who is clean and neat writes more cleanly and neatly than a man who is untidy is obvious.

But the mainspring behind the various indications and the different expressions of likes and dislikes in the formation of individual handwritings is less easy to understand. It is more pictorial and symbolic in nature. To make this sufficiently clear we have to go into the nature of symbols, which is sometimes disclosed by the language itself, sometimes by the ideographic systems of writing, sometimes by the modern psychological science of expression, analysis of dreams, folklore and symbols, psycho-analysis, the study of physiognomy and the psychology of the body and gestures.

As to ideographic writing, the alphabet which we use is not the common property of all nations. Not only primitive races like the Red Indians, but also highly developed civilizations like the Chinese, use a system of writing in which words are not formed by alphabetic letters corresponding to certain sounds but by pictures representing a word. These pictures are sometimes a simple or primitive sketch of the object—a house in Chinese writing is a sketch of a house, a man a drawing of a man. Sometimes the sketch gives only the important part or main attribute of the whole—a man with a stick in Chinese writing means father. Sometimes it is the drawing of a thing which is known for a particular quality and the picture represents this quality. Thus sun means bright, mother means love.

Sometimes the picture of a certain situation stands

for the event which usually arises out of this situation. Two men in a house means council, two women in a house means a quarrel.

Our languages, as well as our cults, rites, dreams and our unconscious life, are full of such symbols, in which pictures either stand for themselves or another thing of which they are a part or an attribute, or are connected with the situation which relates to the thing for which they stand. We say "things are looking up" and we mean things are getting better, and so on. You will recall that a line of writing which rises is also a symbol of optimism.

Our gestures, in so far as they are not merely the outcome simply of physical movements, are also of a symbolic nature and paint, so to speak, our inner thoughts and ideas in the air. When we say somebody takes something, the accompanying gesture, if we make one, depicts the taking and may go as far as making the movement as if to put the object in our own pocket. As we have seen in the sketches illustrating the T stroke, the symbolic nature of handwriting works in the same way.

In exceptional cases, pictures are drawn to represent the actual object the writer has in mind. Sample 98 shows the capital letter N of a signature. When I saw this letter it struck me that it was very similar to the sign which the Chinese use for the word house. As the signature of a man is, in his own mind, the expression of his personality, I felt that this man's whole dreams and imagination about himself must be closely connected with a house. It was confirmed by the writer who a few days before was asked by his wife what he considered to be the most important of all his plans and hopes. He answered "To build a house for myself and my family. But it must be a house made exactly as I want it".

In some cases the object stands for the attribute, the quality. The dot on the *i* formed like a watching eye indicates the faculty of observation.

In another signature (see Sample 97) I found the capital S of the signature formed almost exactly like a walking stick, the symbol of the pilgrim. It belongs to a man who, unlike the one above who wants to settle down in his own house, says of himself that he lives as it were in the waiting room of a railway station, his trunks packed and ready to go.

Pulver reproduced the signature of Marat, the blood-stained hangman of the French Revolution, which clearly shows a rope and dagger. The signature of Talleyrand looks like a moving snake.

But symbols of such an obvious character are very rare. It would be dangerous and prejudicial to serious graphological research to lay too much emphasis on this or to seek it out where it does not exist. In the same way many half-educated followers of psycho-analysis pretend to find sexual symbols everywhere.

Symbols connected with professional experience or inclination are more frequent. They tell you that the writer either has a liking or an inclination for the profession or activity in question, or that he is actually taking part in it. But Jacoby, who did much research work in this line, found that only about a fifth of the handwritings of professional men show these symbols—and these were all men who enjoyed their profession. Thus you find notes and musical keys in the writing of musical persons, paragraph signs in the writing of members of the legal profession, shorthand signs in the writing of shorthand writers, printed characters in the writing of printers, publishers and commercial artists, pictures of scissors and threads in the writing of tailors, figures in the writing of accountants, economists and so on. Jacoby goes further and develops these symbols in

the direction of numerology, mythology and astrology;
but I do not follow him as far as that.

The symbolism of sexual imagination as well as the
disguise of its symbols behind ceremonials and dreams
has become commonplace following Freud's discoveries. Chinese writing uses sexual symbols, as for
instance the sketch of a female organ as the sign of the
word woman. The researching graphologist will find
these symbols also in handwriting, from the whips and
daggers in the handwriting of masochists to the more
drastic symbols in the handwriting of prostitutes,
homosexuals and others.

But all these extreme pictorial symbols are very
occasional and, as it cannot be pointed out too often,
are not found in all cases. They form a distinct link
between graphology and the psychology of the unconscious and of expression. I have already pointed out
that the lunatic often produces a picturesque writing
style of his own, a one-man alphabet, unintelligible to
others who have no access to his thoughts.

The symbolic in the basic signs of graphology,
direction, extension, layout and elaboration, springs
from two sources: individual experience of space and
extension, and individual behaviour in occupying this
space.

Whether you stay put, run or fly, whether you
restrict and discipline your movements or move freely,
whether you look forward or backward, whether up
or down, whether your gestures are round and open, or
stiff and angular or merely conventional, your experience and perspective of the world and of your position in it will always find its symbolical expression in
your writing. So will your personal theory and experience of the easiest and most desirable system of
mastering the problems of work and life.

To sum up: graphological research will start by the

comparison of handwritings of persons with known characters and by finding what characteristics they have in common as an empirical basis for new discoveries. Then, by studying technological, physical and biological pre-conditions of the movements and gestures fixed by the writing, it will be able to reconstruct these movements and gestures. Thirdly, by studying the features obviously related to intellectual and educational spheres and social habits, the graphologist will be able to grasp the intellectual and social background to the individual handwriting. And finally, graphology will be able to rely on the symbolical and ideographical interpretation of the writing as explained in the previous chapters.

This finishes the chapters of the book dealing with the theory of graphology. Later chapters will be concerned with graphological practice, its different applications and the way in which analyses are worked out. This will be, of course, within the confines of the limited purposes of this book.

However, I do not wish to close this discussion without mentioning that in order to restrict myself to essentials I have been compelled to leave out many important and interesting sidelines; among these are criminal, sexual and medical graphology, children's handwriting, the means of detecting forged handwriting, the differences between natural and artificially acquired handwritings and also a more elaborate working out of the different meanings of the same basic elements in handwriting and of the individual shaping of letters.

CHAPTER VII

THE WORKING OUT OF AN ANALYSIS

IN the early days of graphology, analysis consisted merely of summing up the writer's qualities indicated by definite signs, signs which had only one meaning. It remained to a large extent thus in the French school. Upright writing according to Rougemont means reasonableness. So, if someone writes upright he must be reasonable.

It was here that Klages, and others who based themselves on his teachings, broke away. As, according to Klages, the basic elements of handwriting all show a double meaning, the analysing graphologist has to make up his mind which of the two meanings applies to the specific handwriting. Klages' solution of the problem was the introduction of the criterion of the "form standard" of the particular writing. According to his teaching the two qualities indicated by the same element of writing were simply the two sides, the good side and the bad side, of the same tendency, linked together like the two sides of a medal.

Large writing means a tendency to greatness and magnanimity. It also means a tendency to lack of realism, boasting, lack of consideration. Which quality is then prevalent in the writer? Klages' answer is: it depends on the general standard, on the "form degree" of the handwriting of the particular writer. If this standard is high, if the writing shows that the writer on the one hand is full of vitality, talent and spontaneity and on the other hand has the power and skill to harmonize all these latent qualities and to create an individual and rhythmic style of writing, then his formstandard is high and in the majority of cases every element has to be taken as a good sign, the higher quality of the tendency. Thus, if the writer writes large and the "form degree" is high it means that he is a personality of greatness and magnanimity. On the other hand if the form standard is low, either because the writing shows no signs of spontaneity or originality or because it shows that the writer lacks the discipline, vigour and skill to master his divergent and conflicting motives and to harmonize them, then each writing tendency has to be explained within the meaning of the lower quality. So, if such a writer writes large, you have to assume that he overestimates and dramatizes himself, boasts, bullies and lacks consideration and a sense of realities.

Klages introduced five degrees of formstandard. He gave, however, no fixed rules for classifying handwriting into these five degrees. General experience, practice, comparison and intuition have to serve as the basis of judgment and classification. Vitality, originality and harmony are the main indications of a high degree of handwriting. Banality, weakness and lack of co-ordination are the chief signs of a low degree of "formstandard".

Just to give you some samples: Sample 118 would be formstandard 1, the highest. Sample 119 would be formstandard 2. Sample 120 would be formstandard 3. Sample 46 would be formstandard 4. Sample 122 would be formstandard 5, the lowest.

Among Klages' followers, Saudek, who consistently tried to replace pure intuition by fixed technical rules, accepted the form degree. He used seven degrees as a basis of analysis, but based them on three elements as main characteristics:

   (i) Quickness, as an indication of spontaneity.

   (ii) Spacing, as an indication of intelligence.

    (iii) Originality in forming letters, as an indication of
        originality.

As Saudek considered spontaneity and its graphological
sign of quickness the most important element in judging handwriting, especially British handwriting, he
composed an elaborate table with all the characteristics
of quick and slow writing, including neutral signs which
can be found in both.   His pupils, especially Brooks,
elaborated and popularized his teaching.   Brooks de-
clared that there are no definite signs in writing at all,
neglecting all the remarkable discoveries of the French
school in this direction, and endeavoured, by elaborat-
ing a few basic elements, especially the element of
quickness, to cover 80 per cent. of all handwritings.
This is of course another extreme as one-sided as the
reliance on definite signs only.

    Pulver has not so far written a book about the process
of analysis itself, considering this premature until he has
published everything on the basic elements, which have
to be considered when analysing; but the way he
approaches the problem makes his technique of analysing very clear.   He accepts Klages' statement that each
basic element has more than one meaning, but he enlarges it roughly, as follows.   It is not true that each
element has two meanings only, which correspond to
the good and bad side of the same tendency.   The
graphological elements have many more meanings,
each meaning relating to a particular sphere of the
human world.   The form degree does not definitely
decide whether the good or bad side of a certain tendency applies to the writer's personal qualities.   All the
sides of a tendency, the good as well as the bad ones,
may co-exist in the same personality. Every personality
can harbour both good and bad tendencies, and still more
the good and bad potential developments of the same
tendency. Which qualities and tendencies are dominant

cannot be exclusively judged by the general standard of
the writing, but only by carefully checking up each
graphological element and sign with corresponding
elements and signs in the same writing. Not even that
is enough. Every element has to be considered anew in
a different sphere of human nature, spiritual, biological,
social, material, sexual, and has to be checked with
other corresponding elements and signs in the same
sphere.

Here we come to the main point, in which analysis
up till now has been found wanting—in my opinion,
the main reason why graphology has not yet achieved
the public support it deserves, especially in this country.

The analysis techniques given in popular text-books
up to now, whether of this school or that, have been of a
rather haphazard, journalistic or historic nature, not
conforming to the many sides of human personality.
This kind of analysis merely satisfies curiosity and gives
a superficial description of a human being, as a quick
look into a mirror reveals some *prima facie* striking
feature. But this is not enough. If you say of a man
than he is cultured, but excitable, very sensual and un-
balanced, you say a lot, but you do not say enough.
You give no indication of the kind of work he is able to
do, whether he is truthful or a liar, whether he wants to
travel or to settle down, whether his sensuality makes
him an artist, whether it works out in the normal
sexual way or in some perverted form.

We are seen differently by different people; by our
doctor who knows our stomach, by our club fellows
who know our manners, our business friends who know
our reliability, our banker who knows what we spend,
our teachers and office colleagues who know our
capacity and technique of working, our wives who
know something of our temper and our private lives.

If graphology is to achieve its place, it should not

merely give a brief picture of what the graphologist sees at first sight or what is interesting to him, but must try to satisfy and answer the questions of all these people with their different view points as well as of the writer himself, who is concerned with both his objective and subjective position in the world.

In order to facilitate the more systematic working out of the characterological side of analysis, I have put together groups of qualities in different spheres of life, which the graphologist has to look for one by one, when working out an analysis:

NATURAL BASIS OF PERSONALITY: Vitality, Health, Energy, Willpower, Originality, Special Gifts or Deficiencies.

INTELLIGENCE: Clear-mindedness, Quickgrasp, Logic, Co-ordination, Intuition, Imagination, Memory, Faculty of Combining Thoughts.

GENERAL INCLINATION: Spiritual, Idealistic, Social, Realistic, Material, Balanced.

ARTIFICIAL BASIS OF PERSONALITY: Social Background, Education, Manners.

BASIC OBJECTIVE QUALITIES: Genuineness, Sincerity, Honesty, Sympathy, Indifference, Resentfulness, Brutality, Self-confidence, Lack of Self-confidence.

BASIC SUBJECTIVE QUALITIES: Harmony, Conflict, Split Personality.

INDIVIDUAL PERSPECTIVE: Looking forward, Looking Backward, Living in the Present.

SOCIAL TENDENCIES: Introvert, Extravert, Independent, Altruistic, Egotistic, Trustfulness, Distrustfulness, Anti-social and Criminal.

DEGREE OF DEPENDENCY ON OTHERS.

SOCIAL BEHAVIOUR: Kindness, Friendliness, Modesty, Degree of Reserve, Diplomacy, Critical Tenden-

cies, Aggressiveness, Quarrelsome Nature, Boastfulness, Arrogance, Self-Display, Bossiness, Despotism, Lying, Deceit, Jealousy, Frankness, Rude-
ness, Confidence, Communicativeness, Talkativeness, Obtrusiveness, Obstinacy.

APPROACH TO MONEY: Economical, Mean, Magnanimous, Spendthrift.

TEMPER: Calm, Hot-tempered, Changing Moods,
Optimist, Pessimist, Phlegmatic.

PERSONAL STANDARD OF HAPPINESS: Happy, Balanced, Harmonic, Conflicting Tendencies, Depressed, Hypochondriac, Melancholic, Cheerful
nature, Inspired, Maniac.

SPECIAL PROFESSIONAL ABILITIES, INCLINATIONS AND
TALENTS: Musical talent, Manual Skill, etc.

WORKING QUALITIES: Faculty of leadership, Ability
to organize one's time, General qualities of Organization, Disposition and Co-ordination, Intellectual Grasp, Faculty of Observation, Enterprise,
Memory, Diligence, Good Starter, Good Finisher,
Steady Worker, Faculty of Arranging, of Display,
and of Persuasion, Accuracy, Tidiness, Application and Concentration, Technical Skill, Weakness, Slowness, Laziness, Attention to Detail,
Planning, Power of Subordination and Faculty of
Working with Others.

MORAL QUALITIES: Discipline, Kindness, Sincerity,
Honesty, Self-Sacrifice, Reliability.

SPECIAL TASTES: Food, Drink, Dress, Fancy, the
Arts, Settler, Traveller, Spender.

SEXUAL PECULIARITIES: Degree of sensuality and
sexuality. Repressions, Complexes and Perversions,
Impotence.

ABNORMAL STATE OF MIND: Fool, Megalomaniac,
Idiot, Melancholic, Hypochondriac, Hysterical,
Paranoiac.

If you analyse in this way, the same graphic elements may disclose good qualities in one direction and bad ones in another. A man who writes large may be inconsiderate and boastful in his behaviour, but he may have qualities of leadership in his profession. A man who writes upright may be independent in his thinking and in his professional capacity, he may be even-tempered, but also be indifferent socially and lazy as a worker. But how can one say whether he is lazy and indifferent? This must be carefully checked with other handwriting elements such as slowness, degeneration of upper and underlengths, weakness of pressure, neglected writing. Here and everywhere in doubtful cases the general formstandard also comes in.

The next chapter takes the form of a table, compiled in order to show what you have to look for, if, after a general analysis, you are still in doubt about certain qualities of the writer.

CHAPTER VIII

WHAT TO LOOK FOR

GENERAL

VITALITY: Fluid, quick writing, normal or strong pressure, no breaks and amendments, large writing, rhythmic writing.

GOOD HEALTH: Look for the same things as for vitality.

BAD HEALTH or

LACK OF VITALITY: Weak writing, small writing, slow writing, weak pressure, or very heavy pressure combined with low general standard, breaks and "trembling" features, amendments, descending lines, abnormalities.

ENERGY AND WILLPOWER: Signs of vitality combined with regular writing, simplified writing, large writing.

ORIGINALITY: Original forming of letters, either by simplification or additions, full writing, pasty writing of high general standard.

SPECIAL GIFTS

ARTISTIC MIND: Pasty writing, full writing.

MUSICAL MIND: Writing of notes and musical keys.

IMAGINATION: Full writing.

INTUITION: Disconnected writing of high standard. Pasty writing, full writing.

SPECIAL DEFICIENCIES

PHYSICAL WEAKNESS: Weak pressure. No crossing of the "*t*" in the case of round writing. Descending lines.

LACK OF MEMORY AND
MENTAL BLACK-OUTS: Large breaks inside words,
leaving out of letters and words.

BAD NERVES: Trembling features, irregular and non-
rhythmic writing.

EXCITABILITY: Writing with a heavy slope to the
right, irregular size of letters *t* stroke sloping upwards, first letters of words with a long rising
stroke.

HYPOCHONDRIA: Amendments, small writing.

DEPRESSED CHARACTER: Small writing, weak or too
heavy pressure, descending lines, disconnected
writing, large spacing, no starting strokes.

SUICIDE TENDENCIES: The signs of depression, combined with a stroke through the ego (crossing out
of own signature) signature placed to the extreme
left.

MENTAL DEFICIENCIES

HYSTERIA: Thread connection inside words.

MEGALOMANIA: Over-large writing.

PARANOIAC CHARACTER: Unusual and unintelligible
forms of letters, pictures instead of words, repetition of words or leaving out of words or parts of
words, connection of whole sentences without
spacing, mounting lines, using different coloured
inks in the same manuscript.

INTELLECTUAL QUALITIES

INTELLIGENCE: Good lay out, clear spacing, simplification, letters becoming smaller at the end of
words, connection of *t* cross and dot over the *i* with
the previous or following letter, quick writing.

CLEARMINDEDNESS: Good spacing.

QUICK-WITTEDNESS: No starting strokes or other ad-
justments at the beginning of words.   Quick
writing.

LOGIC: Connected writing.

SCIENTIFIC MIND and

FACULTY OF COMBINING THOUGHTS: Simplification. Connecting of dots over the *i* or the cross over the *t* with the preceding or following letters.

FACULTY OF OBSERVATION: Dots over the *i* like "watching eyes", disconnected writing.

FACULTY OF JUDGMENT: Upright writing.

FACULTY OF CO-ORDINATION: Good layout and spacing, regular writing, large underlengths.

GENERAL INCLINATION

SPIRITUAL AND IDEALISTIC: Large writing, dominance of upperlengths.

SOCIAL: Dominance of middlelengths, writing sloping to the right, extension of end strokes.

MATERIAL: Dominance of underlengths, left tendencies.

BALANCE: Regular, rhythmic writing.

REALISM: Small writing, dominance of underlengths, disconnected writing.

ARTIFICIAL INFLUENCES ON PERSONALITY

SOCIAL BACKGROUND: Margins and spacing. Ample means large social background, narrow means small.

EDUCATION: Simplification, speed, skilled forming of letters, ends of words decreasing, printed characters.

MANNERS: Constancy of margins, clear spacing.

BASIC INDIVIDUAL QUALITIES

GENUINENESS AND SPONTANEITY: Speed, simplification.

SINCERITY: Garland connection, increasing size of letters in words, broad writing.

KINDNESS: Garland connection.

DISCIPLINE: Regular writing.

HONESTY: Lack of left tendencies in combination with signs of sincerity, genuineness and discipline.

SYMPATHY: Sloping to the right.

RESENTFULNESS: Angular writing, small writing, sharp writing, lean writing.

SELF-CONFIDENCE: Large writing, broad writing, quick writing.

LACK OF SELF-CONFIDENCE: Small writing, weak pressure, descending lines, slow writing, degeneration of middlelengths, low crossing of the *t* and dotting of the *i*.

SOCIAL TENDENCIES

EXTRAVERT: Sloping to the right.

INTROVERT: Sloping to the left.

INDEPENDENCE: Upright writing, arcade connections, crossing of the *t* going back and overhead.

ALTRUISTIC: Right tendencies, extending the end strokes, *t* cross covering the whole word.

EGOTISTIC: Left tendencies. Writing sloping to the left. Very large, very broad or very narrow writing. Covering strokes and the various signs of despotism and coercion.

ASOCIAL AND CRIMINAL: Strong characteristics of egotism combined with the writing characteristics of mental or physical weakness, lack of discipline, brutality, resentfulness or sexual perversity.

DEGREE OF MENTAL DEPENDENCE ON OTHERS

INDEPENDENCE: Upright writing.

PRIDE: Capital letters getting smaller.

SOCIAL BEHAVIOUR
FRIENDLINESS: Garland connection.

CALMNESS: Upright writing.

SHYNESS: Narrow capital letters.

MODESTY: Small writing, small capital letters.

OBTRUSIVENESS: Small spacing between words, inter-mingling of lines, small margins, no paragraphs.

OBSTINACY: Hooks, angular writing.

QUARRELSOMENESS: Starting stroke beginning below the level of the letter and rising, mounting *t* crosses.

AGGRESSIVENESS: Sharpening *t* cross, sharpening of loops.

BRUTALITY: Heavy pressure, *t* cross getting thicker at the end.

MALICIOUSNESS: Sharp small writing.

FRANKNESS: Ends of words mounting.

RESERVE: Large distance between words: upright writing or writing sloping to the left.

DIPLOMACY: Arcade connection.

PRIMITIVENESS: Unskilled forming of letters, inter-mingling of lines, mounting words.

BOASTFULNESS: Large capital letters.

ARROGANCE: Capital "M" with strokes decreasing in size.

BLUFFING: Vertical crossing of the letters capital H and small *x*.

IMPUDENCE: Same characteristics in low standard handwriting.

DESIRE TO IMPRESS, CUMBERSOMENESS, THE BUSY-BODY: Elaboration of capital letters and the first letters of words, superfluous strokes.

BOSSINESS: Large broad *t* crosses on the top of the letter, loop of the letter *g* in the form of a triangle. The latter is a special sign of domestic tyranny.

LYING: Arcade connections combined with left tendencies and slow writing.

GREED: Ends of words and *t* crosses ending like a claw.

CHEATING: Combined characteristics of lying and greed.

JEALOUSY: Exaggeration of some small letters inside words, mostly the letter *a*.

TOUCHINESS: The same as for jealousy, also upstroke of loop in the letter *g* or *h* broken with loop leaning to the right.

REVENGE: Loops pointed at the top and bottom.

FLATTERY: Strokes at the ends of words going to the left and ending with a stop.

TALKATIVENESS: Broad writing.

DISTRUST: Narrow writing, covering strokes.

MOODINESS: Irregular writing, lines going up and down.

HABIT OF BREAKING OFF RELATIONS ABRUPTLY: Words ending without end strokes to the right.

WORKING QUALITIES

FACULTY OF LEADERSHIP: Large writing, regularity, strong pressure.

ORGANIZATION: Good general outlay and long underlengths.

POWERS OF DISPOSITION AND CO-ORDINATION: Good spacing, good general outlay.

QUICK INTELLECTUAL GRASP: Simplification, words beginning without starting strokes.

FACULTY OF OBSERVATION: Break after capital letters, "watching eyes."

ENTERPRISE: Large, broad, quick writing.

IMAGINATION: Full writing.

MEMORY: Connected writing.

DILIGENCE: Large starting strokes, writing slanting to the right.

GOOD STARTER: No starting strokes, good outlay.

STEADY WORKER: Regularity.

GOOD FINISHER: End of sample of handwriting more regular than the beginning.

BUSINESS MIND: "Money grip" that is the claw (see greediness) combined with the characteristics of organization.

FACULTY OF DISPLAY: Enriched writing.

TOUGHNESS: Knots in the letters *f* and *t*.

ACCURACY: Exact dotting of the *i*, writing commas exactly.

TIDINESS: Clean, tidy writing.

ABILITY TO CONCENTRATE: Simplified writing, no loops in the underlengths.

WEAKNESS AND TIREDNESS: Low pressure, small writing, no crossing of the *t*, descending lines.

LAZINESS: Slow, upright writing, neglected writing.

FACULTY FOR DETAILED WORK: The same as for accuracy.

SUBORDINATION: Small writing, low crossing of the *t*.

FACULTY OF WORKING WITH OTHERS: Absence of graphological signs of intolerance, quarrelsomeness, obstinacy and malice.

MORAL QUALITIES

DISCIPLINE: Regular handwriting.

KINDNESS: Garland connections.

SINCERITY: Garland connections, lack of left tendencies.

HONESTY: Lack of left tendencies and high standard handwriting.

SELF-SACRIFICE: Writing sloping to the right.

RELIABILITY: Regularity combined with the graphological signs of sincerity and accuracy.

SPECIAL TASTES

FOOD: Pasty writing.

DRINK: Pasty writing with trembling downstrokes.
DRESS: Neat and enriched writing.
READING: Printed letters.
SETTLER: Square writing.
TRAVELLER: Broad writing.
SPENDER: Wasting of space.
SEX: Exaggeration of underlengths.

CHAPTER IX

A SAMPLE ANALYSIS

THE technical preconditions of writing have been extensively dealt with by Saudek. For the purposes of this book it is sufficient to mention that in order to make an analysis, the sample to be examined should have been written in normal conditions, i.e. not in a train, or not in an unusual state of excitement or depression. There should be at least a full·page of writing so that one can see if the characteristics have changed at the end of the page compared with the beginning. At all costs the sample page of handwriting should *not* be written specially for the occasion, as in these circumstances the writer is much more writing-conscious. Copying from books, especially poetry, and writing on lined paper should never be used. Nor should writing be accepted on narrow slips of paper or cards which compel the writer to alter the normal size of his writing.

A genuine letter, written in normal writing circumstances and not for the special purpose of examination, is the most desirable material for analysis.

Three things must be made known to the analysing graphologist before the examination of the writing is begun:

(i) Approximate age (e.g. between forty and fifty).

(ii) Sex.

(iii) The country in which the writer learnt to write.

It may seem strange that, although the most subtle characteristics can be discerned from handwriting, leading graphologists make errors of up to 60 per cent. in ascertaining sex and age. The reason is that psychologically, age and sex are relative. There are male and female mental qualities in each human being, there are boys of fifty and old men of twenty. One does not grow up strictly according to the calendar.

If you know sex and age, it tells you a lot if a boy has the writing of an old man, or if a woman's handwriting looks very masculine to you. But it is absolutely indispensable that these two facts be known before you begin the analysis.

To know where the writer has learnt to write is useful because, as has already been stated, the copybook form of handwriting is different in different countries. If you want to assess the variations from the copybook form, you must be aware of the standard pattern. It also helps to judge correctly slowness and mistakes, if you know whether the writer is writing in his native language or not.

The analysis of the writing of very old people who are already in a state of decay or of very young children whose character is still in the stage of being built up, or of handwriting written in an unusual state of mind should be refused at any rate by the student graphologist. The beginner should also refuse any handwriting to which he feels no personal approach.

Now let us demonstrate how a real analysis is done. For a sample we are taking the letter reproduced on page 99 (Sample 123). This, we are told, is written by an Englishman about fifty years old. Let us first form a general impression.

1. There is great regularity in the distance between the margin and the beginning of the lines.

2. There is also a clearly marked distance between words and also between the lines.

3. There is a distinct tendency to avoid sharp

angles, shown by an almost constant garland connection.

It should be noted that these three features seem to
be the most striking points in the writing. Therefore
the reasons for them must represent the most important features of the writer's character.

Let us also get a general impression of the standard
of the writing. It is certainly a high one. The writing
looks genuine and natural as well as original and
personal.

Now let us read the letter. We will note that in one
sentence ("drink together on the strength it") the word
"of" is left out.

After this preliminary glance, let us now make a
systematic graphological analysis:

SIZE OF THE LETTERS: Rather small with preponderance of the middle lengths. See the word "young",
second line from bottom.

WIDTHS: Rather broad. See the word "view" second
line.

ANGLE OF WRITING: Upright.   } Consistent
GENERAL OUTLAY: Good and clear.   throughout
DISTANCES: Extremely marked.   the whole
FORM OF CONNECTION: Garland.   }   text.

TEMPO OF THE WRITING: Elements of quickness (gar-
lands, dotting of the *i*, crossing of the *t*, end-
strokes simplification) preponderant but also some
elements of slowness (upright writing, breaks).

DEGREE OF CONNECTION: Changing with some large
and sudden breaks inside words. See the word
"temperature" second line from top.

FORMING OF LETTERS: Simplified throughout the
whole text.

PRESSURE: Just normal, traces of pastiness. See the *e*
in temperature.

beside me and 4 whiskeys inside me.
The view is gorgeous; the temperature just
right; I'm going home in ten days
and everybody loves me including you
apparently. So to graphologise on
this evidence might be misleading.

I feel generous though I'm normally

---

few drinks together on the strength
it!
I see you are in the same flat.

One day soon, I will call to discover
how old and young are progressing

Thanks for your kind letter and

DIRECTION OF LINES: Regular. ⎱
REGULARITY: Rather regular and de-⎰ Throughout
  cidedly rhythmic.   the whole
COVERING OF SPACE: Rather full. ⎰   text.
RIGHT AND LEFT TENDENCIES: Almost no left
  tendencies.
SPECIAL FEATURES: Formation of the small *e* in two
  arcs open to the right. See the words "beside" and
  "me", first line.

On this graphological evidence let us now build up
a picture of the writer's character grouped into:
    (i) Social Attitude.
   (ii) Gifts and Inclinations.
  (iii) Personal Likes and Dislikes.

(i) SOCIAL ATTITUDE

The constant distance between the left margin and
the beginning of the lines and the regularity of the
writing indicates a constancy in behaviour, discipline
and excellent manners. The lavish spacing between
words and between lines shows that the writer is not
handicapped by strong monetary restrictions. The upright angle of the writing indicates independence and a
calm, phlegmatic, well-tempered attitude. The garland
connections show friendliness and kindness. The
simplification of the writing shows a tendency to lack
of pomposity. The exaggerated spacing between words
shows a strong feeling of intellectual and perhaps social
discrimination. This last sign taken with a few superfluous slopes (see the first *t* in the word *letter* in the last
line) indicates slight vanity and prejudice, a degree of
snobbery, which sometimes leaves the writer himself
with a feeling of loneliness and inner isolation. The
broadness of the letters and the space he needs are also
indicative of a man who, in spite of being nice and

friendly, even obliging to others, does not like to be bound to them by stringent obligations. The fullness of the writing together with the elegant curves and slopes indicate imagination and a nice sense of humour. The width of the letters shows that in spite of his sense of discrimination and a certain professional taciturnity, which is indicated by the closing and "knotting" of the letter *o*, he can be very communicative and talk freely in private life. He also likes occasional discussions (see upstroke at the start of words). The forming of the middle part of the letter *g* and the extension of the end-strokes shows experience of social routine. The proportion between capital letters and small letters shows lack of any sign of bossiness; nor are there any other signs in his writing indicative of this.

GIFTS AND INCLINATIONS

The clear layout, spacing and distribution shows great clarity of mind, and a faculty for disposition, distribution and planning. These signs taken in conjunction with the simplification of letters show intellectual culture and good education. Some printed capital letters are a sign of the reader. But the outstanding gift of this gentleman is an excellent faculty of observation. It is indicated by the transforming of some of the dots over the *i* into little triangles and arcs opening to the right, which look like a watching eye, but also by a tendency to transform other letters like the downstrokes of the *g*, the *l*, and especially the small *e* into these "watching eyes". The intervals which occur between the capital letter and the rest of the word also point in the same direction. So does the relatively small writing, which indicates realism.

The third outstanding gift is the writer's ability to concentrate on essentials, indicated by simplification as well as by the downstrokes of the *g* which go straight down without strokes or curves. That this faculty of concentration and observation is combined with imagination is shown by the writing being full in spite of simplification.

The absence of any left tendency and any other sign of insincerity shows the writer's honesty.

WORKING CAPACITY

His outstanding gifts enable the writer to undertake work of the highest standard. In executing it he has however to cope with certain limitations. The regularity of his writing shows energy and discipline, but the upright nature of the writing and the fact that the pressure is not too strong, the smallness of the writing, the interruptions and even occasional breaks are signs that his vitality is not without limitations. The writer overcomes this limitation by very wise economy and full utilisation of his strength, which leaves no room for any superfluous work or ambition. While he is a quick thinker, he works more slowly and with discipline. He cannot afford himself to go into every detail (irregular dotting of the *i*). He always tries to improve (note that he amends some letters). This effort to improve has something of hypochondria in it. His memory, under the strain of his effort, also shows occasional deficiencies (split words, omission of words). He is courageous (width of letters) and does not mind dangers, adventure or the effort of travelling (same sign).

PERSONAL TASTES

Some of his likings have already been indicated. His handwriting shows no sign of greed or of commercial tendencies. While not a spender (small size of writing), he always lives up to his social position, has money to enable himself to dress well (slopes) and to travel (widths), which he loves passionately. He does not

mind a drink or two (pasty writing) but is a moderate
eater (lean, evenly forked downstrokes on lower parts
of letters). He likes music (note writing) is a keen
reader (printing), with a sense of colour and a feeling
for art (pastiness, fullness) and likes epic, descriptive
books (widths).

Though he is a little sensual, sex and women do not
play an overriding part in his life (short and simplified
downstrokes).

In order to make the above analysis simpler to
follow, the outstanding points are repeated herewith in
the form of a table.

SIGN	MEANING
Small size of writing.	Limited vitality.
	No bossiness.
Broad writing.	Likes discussions, travelling and descriptive books.
	Courage.
Upright writing.	Independence.
	Good tempered.
	Phlegmatic.
Good layout.	Clearmindedness.
	Faculty of disposition and planning.
	Good manners.
Marked distances.	Intellectual and social discrimination.
	A certain loneliness.
Garland connection.	Friendliness.
Quickness preponderant, but elements of slowness too.	Quick grasp, but planner.
Varying degree of connection and breaks.	Very strained memory. Faculty of observation.

Simplification.	Lack of pomposity.
	Clarity of mind.
	Concentration.
Normal pressure, traces of pastiness.	No outstanding physical reserves.
	Does not mind a drink or two.
Regular direction of lines.	Discipline.
	Constancy of behaviour.
Rather regular and rhythmic writing.	Discipline.
	Routine.
	Genuineness.
Rather full covering of space	Imagination.
	Sense of humour.
No left tendencies.	Honesty.
	No greed or commercial inclinations.
Special formation of small *e*.	Faculty of observation.

PART TWO

THE GRAPHOLOGIST'S ALPHABET

CHAPTER I

THE COPY-BOOK ALPHABET AND THE INDIVIDUAL'S ALPHABET

THE beginning of writing started, not with the alphabet representing sounds, but with pictures representing objects. The individual sketches which initiated this form of communication later developed into agreed sketches, each sketch representing one object, either by picturing the object itself (**bird** for *a bird*) or an attribute characteristic and representative of the object (man with a stick for *father*). Some of these pictorial writings, like the Chinese, developed further by depicting symbols for qualities (sun **for** *bright*) or situations for categories (two women in **one** house for *a quarrel*). Several nations beside **the** Chinese, especially among primitive races, still **use** pictorial writing.

It was the Egyptians, who, after first having invented the pictorial writing of the hieroglyphics, later started something which already approached an alphabet. The Assyrians pictured not an object, but a syllable.

The first nation to invent a real alphabet in which the drawing of a code of letters represented sounds (consonants and semi-vowels) was the great trading nation of early antiquity, the Phœnicians. Phœnician traders from Egypt brought home Egyptian writings, and based on these, the Phœnicians invented a complete alphabet of twenty-two letters, each representing a different sound. The Phœnicians invented not only the alphabet, but also a numerical system in which the letters of the alphabet at the same time represented a certain number.

They also invented money, the currency system which is still the basis of our monetary system.

The Phœnician alphabet, in which the letters had no clear pictorial meaning but were a code and index of sounds, enabled the writer to join these sounds together to words which now presented themselves to the reader as a currency of communication instead of the earlier system of depicting objects.

The Greeks took over the Phœnician alphabet and elaborated it to twenty-six letters, and the Romans took it over from the Greeks. Based on the Greek alphabet (with the exception of a few remaining pictorial systems) with national variations, differences and elaborations, it became the currency of writing of nearly the whole world. In the course of this process it developed in Greece (long before classical times, of course) from writing from the right to the left to a writing system from the left to the right. Later the writing of capital and small letters developed. The numerical system was divided from the alphabet; and with the invention of printing, handwriting and mechanical printing became different. Today, in Europe, and the countries colonized by Europeans, there are five distinctly different alphabets all derived from the Greek and Latin alphabets: the Cyrillic in the Slavic states, in which the Orthodox Church was the main Church; the Greek alphabet in Greece, the Gothic alphabet in Germany; the Gaelic in Ireland; and the Latin in the rest of Central and Western Europe and the countries colonized by Europeans.

But copy-book writing in the different European and American countries is not identical. It differs in almost every country according to national characteristics and traditions, and it differs in the same country at different times, according to the different spirit of the times (*Zeitgeist*).

There is at the moment no unified type of copy-book writing in Great Britain, but rather two distinct styles: block-letter printing and cursive, for which latter some copy-books edited by Mary Richardson in the early years of this century are used in schools. There exists, though a bit out-of-date, a good book for information about the different copy-book styles by F. Victor, published in Berlin in the 1930s and called *The Copy-book Forms of Fifteen Nations*.

For the graphologist the knowledge of the exact copy-book system under which the writer learnt to write is of great importance. If in doubt, he should not hesitate to inquire, as graphology is based on observing deflections from the national style and is likely to be a failure if it is applied without a knowledge of the standard patterns. Saudek, the first great graphologist from the Continent who worked and died in Great Britain, felt very strongly about it, and made the characteristics of national writing a matter of special study. He contended that graphology, as learned in one country, can only be applied in another country if the principles are adjusted to the national form of writing and to the national characteristics of the respective country.

Not only do the national copy-book forms differ, but the writing of each individual differs to a greater or lesser degree. It differs not only from the copy-book style he has learned at school but also from all other handwritings. Why is this? The answer to the question is the very essence of graphological research. The answer is simple to give, but it is complicated to follow up in every detail. The simple answer is: individual handwriting differs from the standard type because the human standard type does not exist and is only a scientific hypothesis. The man who eats so many calories, reaches this or that age, etc., is a hypothesis necessary to economics, statistics, etc. But a living person, even in the most favourable case, can only approach the standard type. No two human beings can ever behave in every respect exactly the same. Therefore, they never write either completely according to standard pattern nor in an exactly identical way. Even the best trained calligraphist's work will in some slight degree differ from the printed copy-book from which he has to copy.

In what way are human beings different? In their bodies, their nerves, their movements, their senses, their minds, their brain and imagination, their talents and background, their education, their antecedents, their traditions, their appearance, their habits, their environments and surroundings, climatic and visual impressions, their health, their images, their tastes, their objectives, their technical means and skill, the degree of resistance they have to fight against, etc. I could fill a whole book with such a catalogue. In the process of writing, that is in shaping letters, all these factors in a personality will play their part. The writers will accept the agreed forms of letters only to the degree which makes communication and understanding possible. And sometimes in the case of children, lunatics, asocials, men who want to hide their personalities, they will either neglect and destroy the forms of letters so far that they are unintelligible or they will form their own "one-man's alphabet" which has significance only to the writer himself. The balance of the wish of the individual to remain in communication with others and his devotion to the separatist and individualist tendency in himself, is the very essence not only of any civilization as a whole, but of the conflict of impulses of everybody's mind.

The currencies of communication, money, language and writing have for that reason always at least a double meaning, and mostly many meanings, for the individual. Money, for example, apart from its agreed use as a medium of buying and selling, will have a different meaning for different people.. For John it will mean the house he wants to buy; for Patricia, frocks and luxury; for Jack, rest and holidays; for Charles, power; and for Isobel, a complex and taboo. For Ernest it will be an argument in his public speeches; for Samuel, gambling on football pools and greyhound racing; for Percy, women, and only for Constance, the theorist, will it mean something abstract—money itself, a frozen token of human relations, a barter instrument for the exchange of goods, savings and services.

Similarly, every word used in the language will fill the mind of the man who reads or hears it with different images. *Red* the colour, *B Flat* the musical note, and *i* the vowel will, first of all, never be seen or heard in a completely identical way by different individuals because their senses of perception each function slightly differently. Exaggerated, *red* may mean bright red for Francis; scarlet to Arthur; wine red to Felix; and carmine to Paul; and the written or spoken word *red* will evoke in Elizabeth's imagination the tapestry she wants for her reception room; in Guy, the picture of his most valued specimen of Great Britain's halfpenny stamp of Queen Victoria; in Anne, the vision of the roses in mother's garden; and in Henry a dream of Mary's golden hair.

This process of our minds in bringing sensations and images together into accentuated words of abstract meaning and then dissolving them again into images of individual subjects is a constant repetition of the building of the Tower of Babel, of the eternal fight between the standard pattern of uniformity, and the inborn human demand for variety. We witness this process daily with the addition of new words to the language, abstract words which still clearly show the concrete subject from which they originated.

Take for instance the word *quisling* which was added to the English language in the last war. Today its commonly accepted meaning is "traitor to his nation from lust for power". For our contemporary generation this word is still full of living content, and the connection with the Norwegian dictator is still clear. In centuries to come it will become only an accepted standard expression for "traitor", and the real Quisling will be forgotten; still later on, human imagination will fill this abstract word again with living content.

In handwriting analysis, this process of the individual's deviation from the copy-book pattern enables us to trace the individual's character which worked out the specific shape into which he altered the form which he learned at school. His initiative and intelligence, his ambition and taste, his vitality, etc., will all emerge from a systematic analysis.

You can read about this in greater detail in the following chapters. I begin by giving a series of small drawings to illustrate the different meanings of various tendencies, in order to help students to memorize them visually.

ך

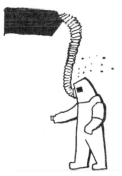

1	Large writing	*Subjectivity, a longing for real or imagined greatness*

2	Small writing	*Realism, modesty, lack of ambition*

3	**Exaggeration of under lengths**	*Emphasis on the material and faculty for organization, also dependence on subconscious instincts*

4   Exaggeration of
     upper length

*Preponderance of intellectual and
spiritual interests*

4 (a) Upper and under
        lengths degenerated

*Self-centred lack of interest in any-
thing outside normal human society*

4 (b) Covering strokes

*Secretiveness. Unwillingness to dis-
close changes in mentality and
behaviour. Tactician*

5   Broad writing   *Social appetite, longing for **increased** living space*

6   Connected writing   *Logical sequence of thoughts, **good** memory, adjustability*

7   Disconnected writing   *Many ideas, intuition, observation, poor adaptability*

8   Enriched writing   *Desire for the impressive and ornamental. Dislike of matter-of-factness.*

9   Simplified writing

Sticking to essentials, objectivity, intelligence, soberness

10   Neglected writing

Carelessness about appearance, lack of consideration

11   Angle to the left

Dislike for social relationships; retreat into a private world

12   Upright angle

Independence, reasonableness

| 13 | Right-angle writing | *Extravert, fondness for the company of others* |

| 14 | Changing angle | *Split personality, conflicting tendencies and loyalties* |

| 15 | Long distances between words | *Clear-mindedness, social discrimination, loneliness.* |

| 16 | Small distances between words | *Lack of social discrimination, obtrusiveness, warmth of feeling.* |

to try

17   Whole words
connected

*Fondness for solving problems, braini-
ness, excess of logicality*

mutual

18   Angular connection

Pugnacity, alertness, hardness

mutnal

19   Arcade connection

Impenetrability, diplomacy

mutual

20   Garland connection

Easy-going kindness and friendliness

21	Wavy line connection	*Versatility, changeability, lack of constancy*

22	Thread connection	*Inability to make decisions, suggestibility, lack of conviction, hysteria*

23	Sharp shaded writing	*Sharp, critical mind, lack of sensuality*

24	**Pasty writing**	*Sensuality*

CHAPTER II

THE FIRST LETTER

THE first letter of a written word is interesting for the graphologist as it shows him the way in which the writer grasps new situations, adjusts himself to new conditions and environments, and generally sets out on a new job of work.

Just as a man entering a room for the first time is always somewhat in the limelight, so the first letter of a written word shows how a person behaves when he feels that interest is focussed on him. Starting to write a word means, translated into the language of the graphologist, simply and plainly, "start". We have to remember that like the cross of the *t*, the dot on the *i*, punctuation and the end-stroke, the starting stroke of the first letter of a word is not connected with the previous word and therefore leaves the writer free to move his pen in the way he consciously or unconsciously wants. As to the degree of quickness in grasping situations and adjustment to new environments, the first letter will show whether the writer begins operations with or without any starting strokes. If he makes a preparatory stroke, it may either go in the direction intended (to the right) like a man who takes a run before jumping, or in a contrary direction to the rest of the writing, revealing the difficulties the writer feels in overcoming his attachment to the past and to some former environment. Almost the same applies to the way in which the writer starts an ordinary job of work. It shows whether he needs time for preparation, whether he is a busybody or fusspot who lacks objectivity, or whether he has quick perceptions and goes to the task without unnecessary delay.

As to the behaviour of the newcomer who feels himself to be in the limelight, it will be clearly shown in the first letter whether the writer behaves naturally or makes an effort to impress and to draw attention to himself, or does just the opposite and tries to be as unobtrusive as possible. In the case where he behaves naturally his real degree of self-assurance, dependence upon the opinions of others, modesty or pride, is revealed as well as his ability to assess new situations. His tact will come out as well as the opposite qualities. From self-dramatization to abject understatement, from natural greatness to natural modesty, all the characteristics are shown in the way in which the first letter is written. The little sketches which finish this chapter make all that quite clear.

It is also of interest to observe at what point on the page the writer starts writing, and how he starts each line. The writer who starts a manuscript right at the top of the page near to the upper edge is unorthodox and unconventional in his approach to new problems and consequently sometimes lacking in tact. The writer who starts at normal height respects conventions. The writer who starts too low overdoes them.

Regarding lines, large margins on the left indicate a high standard of living which does not compel the writer to economize. Small margins combined with narrow writing, indicate intentional over-economy; combined with normal writing they show that the writer comes from an environment which, at least for a time, compelled him to economize; combined with very broad writing it indicates that the writer wants to use every bit of space for himself.

A regular and constant distance from the left margin shows steadiness and discipline of behaviour expressed through good manners. If the margin starts quite narrow and becomes broader it expresses a desire to economize which the writer is not capable of keeping up.   It also shows a tendency to fatigue.   A margin which starts broad and becomes narrower shows that the generosity was only pretended, while the writer really wants to save his pennies.   It also indicates that as a worker he starts casually and becomes more and more industrious as the work proceeds.

A special study should be made of the first letter of a person's signature.   The special importance of the signature lies, as Max Pulver explains, in the fact that it represents to the world the personality of the writer. On the one hand a man is seldom disposed to change his signature, because it has become a kind of stamp and has acquired a certain publicity: on the other, it often remains the expression of an earlier stage of the writer's personality while his ordinary writing has changed.   The difference in the writing of the text and the signature, therefore, is very revealing.   The focus should again be centred on the first letter of the signature.   It indicates by comparison whether the writer has more self-admiration than he admits (if the signature is larger than the text) or less (if the text is larger than the signature).   It also shows whether he is more ambitious than he shows (mounting signature, while the lines of the text do not go upwards).

A special significance is attached to a comparison of the first letter of the Christian name, surname and titles.   It shows the degree of importance which the writer attaches to each of them.

The first letter of the Christian name will be emphasized by people

(a)   who feel strongly about their youth, the time when their surname was unimportant;

(b)   who want to be familiar to everybody under their Christian name;

(c) who for some reason hate their second name, like a married woman who hates her husband and regrets her marriage; people of foreign descent who want to hide the foreign name which gives it away, etc.

These people will often tend to drop the second name in their signature altogether whenever possible.

The first letter of the second name will be emphasized by everybody who

(i) is proud of his name for clannish or other reasons;

(ii) dislikes privacy and wishes to be taken objectively on his personal value.

People like that will sometimes drop their Christian name completely.

The emphasizing of the initial letters of titles shows the inner relationship to this title.

This finishes the theoretical exposition of the first letter, and now let us look at some more ideographical diagrams.

25   First letter very
       narrow

Initial shyness

26   First letter very
       broad

Initial lack of control and forethought

27   First letter enriched
       by a vertical
       ornamental stroke

Impudence, arrogant vulgarity

28   First letter starting
       with an arc far under
       the line and moving
       left and upwards

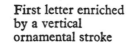

*Broad, appealing gestures and speech.
Actor. Orator*

29 Second part of initial
letter shorter

Ambition

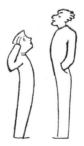

30 End stroke of first
letter extended under
the word

*Conviction of own importance, self-
admiration*

31 Second part of capital
M rising

*Dependence on public opinion and
acknowledgment, the inferiority
complex of the ambitious*

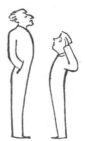

32   Second part of capital
      M descending

Aristocratic feeling, pride, arrogance

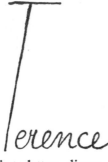

33   First letter dispro-
      portionately high

Fighting against own lack of self-confidence by showing-off, over-compensation of inferiority complex, self-dramatization.

34   Large point at begin-
      ning of first letter, the
      pen resting for a while
      on it

Enjoying of material achievements and pleasures

35   First letter without starting stroke   *Quick calculation, action without preparation*

36   Long starting strokes   *Aggressive and cumbersome preparations, busy-body, fusspot*

37   Nick in first letter   *Touchiness, sensitiveness*

38   End stroke of first letter extended with an arcade to the left

Self-protecting gesture, covering front and back. Avoiding of responsibilities

39   Initial stroke touching the head of the letter

Writer feels a heavy strain in mastering his affairs

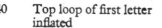

40   Top loop of first letter inflated

Dreamer, muddle-head

41 First letter ending with a lassoo-like stroke

Shrewdness, fixed ideas

42 Little hooks

Persistence, pig-headedness

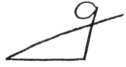

43 Square letter

Interest in building and technical work. Mechanical skill

44 Broad triangular basis

Vanity, with tendency to put everything on a solid material basis

45 Full-simplified, concave arc

A good mixture of vision and realism. Creative and constructive mind, which successfully puts ideas into effect.

46 Letter split into parts

'Odd man out', mixture of many ideas, shrewd, finds it difficult to work on normal lines.

CHAPTER III

THE LAST LETTER

THE last letter of a word and especially its end-stroke are interesting from three points of view:

(i) As with the start, the *t* cross and the punctuation, the end-stroke of the last letter is generally unconnected with the next word and therefore leaves the writer more freedom to move his pen in whichever direction he feels inclined.

(ii) While the attention of the writer is mostly focussed on the beginning of a word he concentrates less on the writing of its end. His true character, the man as he *is* and not as he wants to be or to appear to be, will therefore be much more easily distinguishable from the last letter than from the first. Furthermore, a comparison between the first and last letters will betray the difference between the real character of the writer and the appearance he wishes to create.

For the detecting of disguised or forged writing the study of the last letter is invaluable. While the forger or the man who disguises his handwriting takes the greatest care to change the more obvious parts of the writing, the parts less in the limelight mostly escape his attention. It has, however, to be stated that, as experiment shows, if the angle of the writing is altered by turning it to the left, supposing the amount of pressure and the degree of energy put into the writing remain the same, the end-stroke becomes proportionately shorter the greater the inclination of the angle to the left.

Another aspect of the extending end-stroke is that it is one of the most important signs of quick writing.

As quick writing is a sign of spontaneity, objective thinking and naturalness of behaviour, this aspect of the degree of the extension of the end-stroke has to be taken into account as well.

The degree of speed is another of the indications which enable the expert to catch the forger, as forged handwriting is generally slowly drawn out as compared with the more quickly written original.

Thus an extended end-stroke copied by the forger will mostly, under the glass, show some signs of trembling, breaks and careful drawing instead of the natural flow and the unbroken and spontaneous appearance of a quickly written end-stroke.

There is one more aspect of the study of the last letter of the word, the purely physiological. Writing is a movement of the hand put into motion by a motor activity of the left side of the brain and the effect of the movement is supervised by the eyes. The quickness of the writing is therefore an indication of the writer's impulses, while the regularity, the rhythmic flow and evenness of the writing reveal the degree of control the writer has over his impulses. At no other point, of course, is impulse so difficult to keep under control as where it has to be stopped and then freed again. This is exactly what happens when the writing is interrupted at the end of a word and then resumed at the beginning of the next. Irregularities, slips and errors which occur in the last letter will therefore be very indicative of the writer's co-ordination and control of his movements, implying mastery of his nervous impulses.

(iii) The most important significance of the end-stroke of the last letter is that it reveals the social attitude of the writer.

There is a symbolism of space in writing. The writer always identifies his own present position in the world with the point which his moving pen has attained. To the left of this point lies the past: origin, home, mother, childhood, his individual and private world. To the right lies the future; fellow men and the social world. When the writer in ending a word makes a break and then has to go on, he is faced with a social decision. Shall he stay where he is and move neither back nor forward? Shall he go back into an egocentric and introverted fool's paradise? Or shall he go home like a successful gold-digger to hoard his booty? Can he escape either into intellectual problems, religion and mysticism (above), or into sex, pleasure and the inanimate material world (below)?

Will he try to avoid any decision simply by fading out, or does he not see the decision and the break between the words at all, because to his mind the world is not divided but a single, indivisible problem from beginning to end?

Not only can a person's social inclinations be seen from the way the end-stroke of the last letter of a word is formed, but also his mood, temper and habit.

The childish and frank will end a word differently from the mature and diplomatic man; the hot-tempered, busy and aggressive, differently from the weak, tired and lazy; the obstinate, hard man, differently from the undecided and reluctant. Also the space left between two words will tell you a lot about social background and habits; whether somebody is discriminating, tactful, snobbish, warm-hearted or even importunate.

The little sketches which follow at the end of this chapter will serve better than words to bring home to you the special meaning of the different ways of finishing the writing of a word.

A person's handwriting will scarcely ever show an

invariably uniform manner of ending the last letter.   If
it does, then the social attitude of the writer is very
determined and clear-cut.   In other cases you will have
to check up how often one trend or another occurs and
then, after making sure of the different meanings, you
will be able to assess that the person in question has a
changing attitude comprising all these different trends.

There is a further meaning attached to the way in
which a person finishes his words, his lines and his
manuscripts.   If the writing starts clear and becomes
neglected, if it starts slowly and becomes quicker or
vice versa, if it starts regularly and becomes irregular,
if it starts in a mounting line and then the line declines
or vice versa, it gives you an indication of the evenness
of the working powers of the writer.   This cannot be
demonstrated by single letters but only by a consideration of the whole manuscript.

Two aspects, however, deserve some special study
and attention:

The first of them is the last word and last letter in
the line.   The person who manages to keep an almost
constant margin on the right-hand side of the page
without splitting or compressing words shows an
extremely high degree of comprehension, quick assessment and control of resources, time and space.   The
person who, on the other hand, always has to compress,
to split words or to drop the line shows lack of the
qualities mentioned.

The person who, as illustrated in one of the following
sketches, always tries to fill in the empty space by
extending the end-stroke of the last word in the line,
while he does not extend the end-strokes of other words,
or even by making separate strokes (as in the spaces of a
cheque) is instigated by an unconscious fear of allowing
somebody else to fill up the blank spaces.   These are
the persons who pedantically lock every door and

drawer, and close every window and file. There is a distrust and fear of crime and deception in this attitude.

The person who leaves a large but fairly even margin at the right-hand side of his page likes to live on a large scale, mostly is at a fairly high level in society and is not much concerned about economizing. The person whose last word in the line sometimes approaches the edge of the page, while in other cases is well in from the edge, is of a moody nature, filled with fears, lacks decision and economy of time and money.

The second aspect which is interesting in this connection is how a writer behaves at the end of the page.

If he continues right to the very bottom of the page and compresses words and lines in order to avoid turning over the page until it is inevitable, it indicates that the writer does not like to make decisions and hesitates to start a new page of his life. Such persons are mostly very sentimental as well, and just as they compress much too much at the bottom of a page, they want to indulge much too lavishly in their sentiments.

There is still the writer to consider who, at the end of manuscripts, starts writing across the margins and empty spaces until there is no more room left. If other signs point in the same direction it may indicate lack of decision or over-economy, but the most important meaning is that the writer does not know when to finish and make a clear break and has no time-table at all. He is the sort of person who goes on talking when the matter is already closed, always remembering new points, and in this way wastes his own and other people's time.

Finally, the end of the signature. Many end it— and this is a sign of culture and modesty—completely without any elaboration of the last stroke. Others repeat and sometimes exaggerate the different characteristics of the end-strokes as enumerated.

In many signatures there is an extra elaboration of the end-strokes, even separate underlining strokes of innumerable different kinds.

Underlining in general means an underlining of the writer's own personality. If it is in the form of a wavy line, it shows joy and gaiety. Complicated elaborations always indicate ostentation or artificial originality, a desire to impress, often even vulgarity. There is also a certain desire for security against forgery in it. A lassoo-like end-stroke means, according to the way, degree, and taste in which the lassoo is swung, and in comparison with other tendencies of the same character, different things ranging from poetic tastes, imagination up to shrewdness and cunning, and fixed ideas and obsessions.

An envelopment of the whole signature, looking like a spider's web, is a sign of a shrewd person, who wants to secure himself from any sudden approach from any direction, sitting like a spider in its web. In extreme cases, which have to be checked up with other signs, it reveals persecution mania.

An end-stroke, which goes back and crosses out the signature, is a sign of deep dissatisfaction and even suicidal tendencies, while a full stop after the name marks conventionality and distrust, especially of anybody who does not stick to conventions of the writer's class.

The end of the signature, like the first letter of it, is also most frequently the point where varying symbols are found, if they occur. The signature of the pioneer flyer, Peugeot, which depicts an aeroplane; and the signature of Marat, which depicts a rope and a dagger, are classical examples.

Rosa Baughan, the British pioneer graphologist, reproduces the signature of Oliver Cromwell, which shows the two last *l*'s of the name formed and crossed like a small *t*. "All the signatures but one", she remarks, "have this curious characteristic to the terminating letters of his name." But what is the reason for this peculiar habit? After discovering the pictorial and symbolic character of the writing, there can be little doubt. It is the sign of the Christian cross which was for Cromwell his flag and banner and his inner justification for all that he did. To be regarded as a crusader was his desire. Therefore, he unconsciously wanted to have the symbol of the cross in his signature, representing his official personality. As there was no *t* in his name, which he could cross, his unconscious mind worked in the way described.

Now for the sketches:

47   End-stroke going up and left down over the letter

Distortion of facts

48   End-stroke going up in a rounded arc

Religious, mysticism

49   End-stroke going vigorously down, (Michon's *Coup de Sabre*)

Fighting spirit, hot temper. Unwillingness to talk things over and to compromise. Belief in solution of problems by cutting the knot.

50   End-stroke going up and left and ending in a point

Purposeful flattery

51   Angle changing and becoming upright or left angular at the end of word

Sudden. last-minute change from readiness to be social into keeping others at a distance

52   Last letter with no end-stroke   *Meanness, brusque severance of social relations*

53   Normal end-stroke   *Normal social relations*

53 (a)   End-stroke extended to the right   *Generosity*

53 (b)   End-stroke exaggerated to the right   *Generosity mixed with intolerance*

53 (c) Last down-stroke of last letter not reaching the bottom of the line. (*L'écriture suspendu* of the French)

Concealment of facts, the man who never was a witness to anything, never admits anything, and is always afraid to expose himself before others

54 Letters growing in size at the end of word

Frankness, childishness

55 Letters diminishing in size at the end of word

Diplomacy, maturity

56   **End-stroke going up
and left and roofing
over the word**

Protecting spirit, patronage

57   **End-stroke going back
and left, pointing
against the last letter**

Egotism

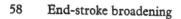

58   **End-stroke broadening**

Brutality

59   End-stroke going deep   *Unwillingness to approach others,*
       down in arcade form   *defensiveness*

60   Under-length of the *G*   *Concentration, fatalism*
       in a s i n g l e v e r t i c a l
       stroke

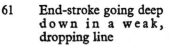

61   End-stroke going deep   *Weakness, tiredness,* nostalgie de la
       d o w n i n a w e a k,   boue
       dropping line

62 End-stroke enrolled to a grasping claw

Greed, egotism

63 End-stroke going up and forming a little loop

Imagination, poetic taste

64 Last letter formed like a cock's comb

Hot temper

65   Last letter of the line extended to the very margin, leaving no space which could be filled up

Distrustfulness, unconscious fear somebody might fill the space up, frequent in writing of persons who lock every cupboard and door behind them

66   Under-length of *G* in two loops

Special degree of vanity, peculiar habits and sentiments

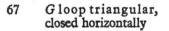

67   *G* loop triangular, closed horizontally

Domestic tyranny, often caused by sexual disappointment

68 Signature completely encircled by end-stroke

Peasant shrewdness, desire to be secure from all sides and trap opponents, spider-like attitude, in extreme cases persecution mania

69 Capital letter of signature deleted by end-stroke

Heavy disappointment, critical attitude against the Ego, suicidal tendencies

CHAPTER IV

THE GRAPHOLOGIST'S ALPHABET

BEFORE I come to the main contents of this part—a collection of typical deviations from the copy-book forms of the alphabet's single letters (capital and small) in the order and sequence of the alphabet, with at least one of the meanings attached to this particular form of letter shaping—I wish to make some final introductory remarks. For some of these meanings graphologists have an explanation, based on the psychology of expression, while some other meanings have only been discovered by observation, but have proved to be correct in practice.

What was stated for the general tendencies of writing is also valid for the single letter; when making an analysis you have to check up with other signs and see whether they back each other up or point in different directions. In my elaboration of a sample analysis (page 96, and following) there is a paragraph on special features. The shaping of single letters, so far as it is not the product and effect of general tendencies, falls under this heading.

In working out an analysis you have to consider each sign not only in combination with other signs, but you have to check it up again and again when considering each side and function of human personality, like working capacity, social attitude, gifts and inclinations, personal likes and dislikes. It may then happen that in that connection you are able to deduce further qualities out of some given to you in the individual case. Take, for instance, the sharpening of the letter "B" at the bottom (example 111, page 156): in connection with working capacity, it points towards the writer working thoroughly and penetrating deeply into the matter in hand. From the point of social relations, you will have to assess that he is a man who finds difficulty in getting over a wrong done to him, and will always relapse into feelings of revengefulness.

As regards general conduct, you will find that he is a man who takes things seriously, and as regards his likes and dislikes, you may come to the conclusion that he dislikes easy-going superficiality. But all that—so complex a science is graphology—still represents only tendencies in certain directions and has again to be checked with other signs and tendencies which point the same way.

It is, of course, superfluous to say that the samples given here, although the number is comparatively large, represent only a small group of types, only those most frequently seen in practice. But if you absorb them and retain them in your visual memory, you may also find the key to other samples.

Unlike most writers who deal with single letters, I show certain characteristic deviations working not only on one, but if possible on several different letters, in order to train the student's eye and to teach him how a particular trend of writing reveals its particular effects in almost every letter made up of the same strokes.

Madame Saint Morand, in her book *Les Bases de l'Analyse de l'Ecriture*, suggests that every letter of the alphabet has a special relationship to some particular feature in human personality: for instance, the letter *B* is an index for altruism or egotism, the letter *D* stands for the inner orientation, the letter *E* shows the degree of personal dignity. Except for the fact that certain letters by their type of extension, are more indicative of sexual and material impulses (like the "under length" letters *g* and *j*) or spiritual and intellectual interests (like the "upper length" letters *l* and *b*), I find Madame Saint.Morand's suggestions very artificial.

What is really important for the student is to be aware of the particular and special movement required for the writing of each individual letter, in order to be able to draw conclusions from the way the writer solves the problem set for him by the particular movement required. In this connection the following basic points about each letter must be noted:

A The small letter *a* according to the copy-book form, compels the writer to slow his movements by forcing him to draw a relatively small circle not higher than the *m* and *n* lines. Drawing a circle means moving the pen 360° to the left in the direction opposite to the continuation of writing. It also requires the writer to make the two ends of the circle to meet again.

B The small letter *b* sets a problem of extension to the top.

C The letter *C* (capital and small) demands the drawing of an arc, open to the right.

D The small letter *d* combines the demand of the small letter *a* and for the extension to the top.

E The capital letter *E* consists of two parts of an arc which have to have the same direction of the angle. The small letter *e* has the smallest circle in the alphabet, which is very easily filled up with ink.

F The small letter *f* in earlier copy-book forms, though not in the most recent one, is the only small letter extending both to top and bottom.

G The small letter *g* is the first letter of the small letters of the alphabet which goes down to the bottom. As the writer has first to draw a circle and has to go slowly, he has some time to prepare the way in which his pen goes down and up again. For that reason the small letter *g* is the most indicative of the writer's approach to material things and expression of sex.

H The capital *H* is revealing in respect of the distance between the two parallel upright strokes. The small letter *h* requires a movement upwards after the down-stroke in order to form the second arcade-shaped part of the letter.

I The small letter *i* is interesting because of the dot, which is unconnected with the previous and following letter and is therefore open to completely individual treatment. The capital *I* is graphically interesting because it is so simple, and because it is similar to the figure 1. It is also remarkable because it is associated with the word *I* and may project the writer's own ideas about himself.

J The capital *J* is interesting because of the semi-arc to the left; the small letter *j*, because of the extension to the bottom and the dot.

K The capital and small *K* are complicated letters, requiring movement in three different directions.

L The small letter *l* is graphologically almost of the same character as the small *b*.

M and **N**. The *M* and *N*, capital and small letters, are very important letters. The small ones are typical arcade letters. Secondly, both capital and small letters consist of two and three parts which should be written on the same height according to copy-book patterns.

O The small letter *o* is interesting in the same way as the small letter *a*.

P The small *p* sets the same problem as *h*, only with the extension to the bottom.

Q The difficulty of the capital *Q* is the stroke which distinguishes it from the capital *O* and the break the writer has to make in order to write this stroke according to standard pattern.

R The small *r* is like a small letter *n* diagonally cut across.

S The small *s* sharpens at the top and then goes down in triangular form and not before it reaches the bottom does the stroke go away in a rolling movement to the left. All this sets a problem to the writer, also the connection with the next letter and the fact that the small letter *s* should not be higher than the other small letters.

T The small letter *t* is the most revealing letter of the alphabet, because of the crossing which is unconnected on both sides and, therefore, allows the writer to move his pen in any direction he wants. The crossing itself also requires a certain robustness of approach.

U The letter *U*, large and small, is a garland letter par excellence.

V The *V*, capital and small, is a standard letter of angular writing.

W The *W* is a kind of inverted *M*.

X The letter X, small or large, leaves the writer the choice between the awkward but gentle cursive form of two arcs, which touch each other but do not cross each other, and the quick simplified but robust block-letter form of two strokes crossing each other.

Y The small letter *y* is a combination of *u* and *g*.

Z The letter *Z*, small or capital, also leaves the choice between the gentle arcs of the cursive form and the sharp angularity of the block letter type.

Close observation of the ways in which a writer solves the problems set by each of these single letters shows all his abilities and deficiencies, his taste and his intellectual powers at work.

Now let us look at some detailed examples of the graphologist's alphabet.

70		Narrow *Shyness*
71		Starting with an Arc to the left *Avarice*
72		Starting with a black point *Enjoying material achievements*
73		Starting with a black point extended to the left *Black spot in the past*
74		Block letter *Culture*
75		Knotted *Toughness, thoroughness*
76		Knotted with a large loop *Pride in own and family achievements*
77		Strokes crossing at the top *Inexact, unconventional*

78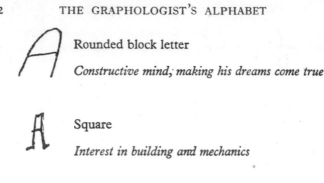

Rounded block letter

Constructive mind, making his dreams come true

79

Square

Interest in building and mechanics

80

Triangular stroke, ending horizontally

Strong reaction against interference

81

Not crossed

Lack of consideration, carelessness

82

Capital letter in form of small letter

Modesty

83

Enrolled

Family man or woman, secretiveness

84

Starting with long stroke extended under the line

Ambitious, quarrelsome, busybody

85

Second stroke shorter

Ambition

86   Rolling to the left

Egoism

87   Several circles

Lives in a world of his own imagination, fixed ideas

88   Starting far extended to the left

Strong attachment to the past

89
a, b   Deleting the letter or stroke descending

Disappointment

90   Middle stroke low

Subordination

91
a, b      Peculiar shape

Exaggerated sex imagination, lowered resistance to excesses and perversions

92   Starting with an angle

Hardness

93
a, b   Open at top

Inaccurate and talkative

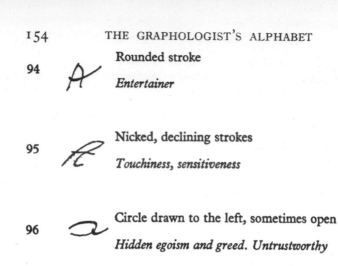

94 Rounded stroke

Entertainer

95 Nicked, declining strokes

Touchiness, sensitiveness

96 Circle drawn to the left, sometimes open

Hidden egoism and greed. Untrustworthy

97 Starting right from the down stroke

Mixture of fussiness, posing and egotism

98 Broad and open

Talkativeness

99 Filled up with ink

Sensuality

100 Open at bottom

Hypocrite, crook

101 With loops

Vanity

102 Square

Mechanical ability

103 Narrow and knotted

Secretiveness, reserve

---

104 Block letter

Reader

105 With claw to the left

Egoist

106 Second arc broad and inflated, extending to the left

Emphasis on own importance

107
a, b
Enrolled

Egoism

108 Narrow

Shyness, reserve

109 Stroke extended at top

Enterprise

110 Elaborated

Vulgar taste, fusspot

111 Angular at bottom

Penetrating mind, determination to get his own way, resentful

112 Peculiar shape

Erotic dreams, lowered resistance to sex exaggerations and perversions.

113 Open at bottom

Wants to know himself

114 Enrolled

Greed, hoarder, egoist.

115 Nicked stroke

Sensitiveness, touchiness

116 Sharpening at top

Resentment

117 Amendments

Hypochondriac, self-tormentor

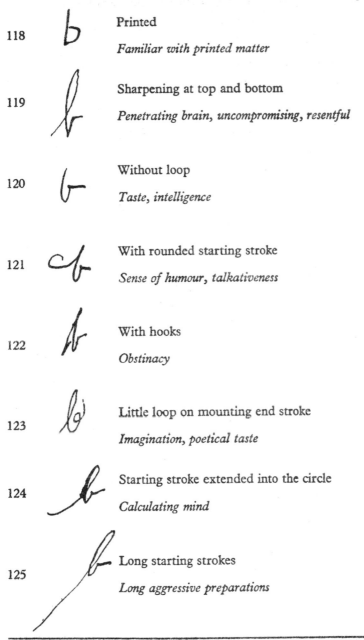

118   Printed

Familiar with printed matter

119   Sharpening at top and bottom

Penetrating brain, uncompromising, resentful

120   Without loop

Taste, intelligence

121   With rounded starting stroke

Sense of humour, talkativeness

122   With hooks

Obstinacy

123   Little loop on mounting end stroke

Imagination, poetical taste

124   Starting stroke extended into the circle

Calculating mind

125   Long starting strokes

Long aggressive preparations

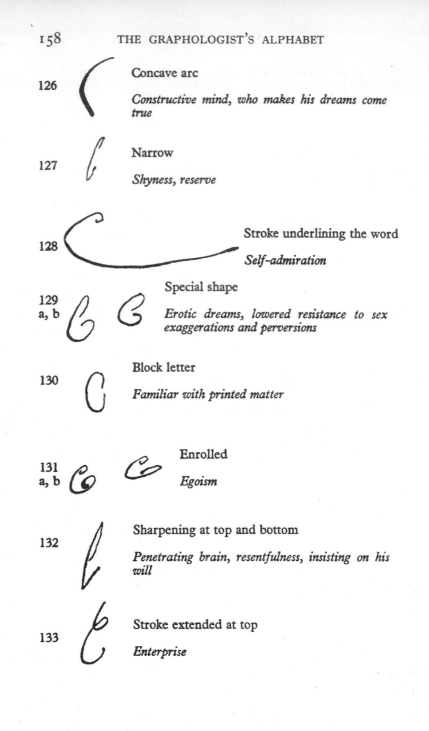

126 Concave arc

Constructive mind, who makes his dreams come true

127 Narrow

Shyness, reserve

128 Stroke underlining the word

Self-admiration

129 a, b Special shape

Erotic dreams, lowered resistance to sex exaggerations and perversions

130 Block letter

Familiar with printed matter

131 a, b Enrolled

Egoism

132 Sharpening at top and bottom

Penetrating brain, resentfulness, insisting on his will

133 Stroke extended at top

Enterprise

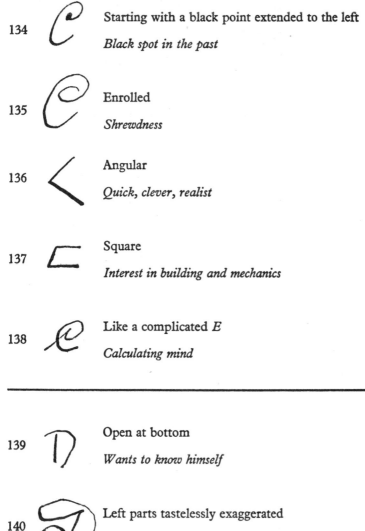

134　Starting with a black point extended to the left
Black spot in the past

135　Enrolled
Shrewdness

136　Angular
Quick, clever, realist

137　Square
Interest in building and mechanics

138　Like a complicated *E*
Calculating mind

139　Open at bottom
Wants to know himself

140　Left parts tastelessly exaggerated
Vulgarity

141　Written in two parts
Individualism, lack of adjustment

142 Second arc broad, with extended stroke

Underlining of own importance

143 Block letter

Simplification, intelligence

144 With claw to the left

Egoist

145 Particular shape

Erotic dreams, lowered resistance to sex excesses and perversions

146 Stroke extended at top

Enterprise

147 Upper length extended

Respect for spiritual values, integrity

148 a, b Open at top and broad, or in two parts

Talkativeness

149 Simplified with arc to the left

Taste

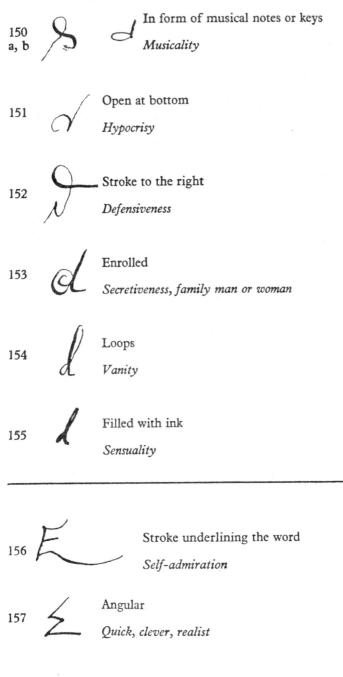

**150
a, b**   In form of musical notes or keys

Musicality

151   Open at bottom

Hypocrisy

152   Stroke to the right

Defensiveness

153   Enrolled

Secretiveness, family man or woman

154   Loops

Vanity

155   Filled with ink

Sensuality

---

156   Stroke underlining the word

Self-admiration

157   Angular

Quick, clever, realist

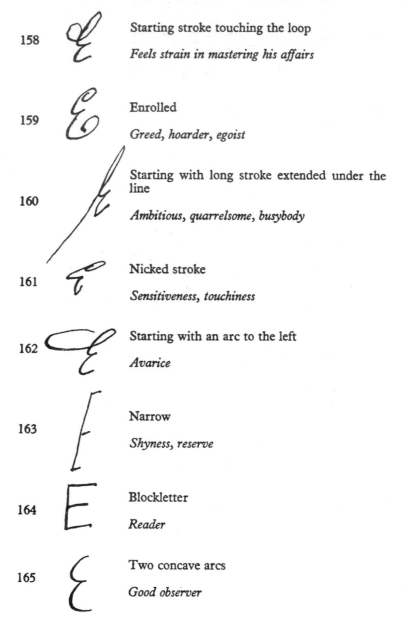

158 Starting stroke touching the loop

Feels strain in mastering his affairs

159 Enrolled

Greed, hoarder, egoist

160 Starting with long stroke extended under the line

Ambitious, quarrelsome, busybody

161 Nicked stroke

Sensitiveness, touchiness

162 Starting with an arc to the left

Avarice

163 Narrow

Shyness, reserve

164 Blockletter

Reader

165 Two concave arcs

Good observer

166    Particular shape

Erotic dreams, lowered resistance to sex excesses and perversions

167    Going up and down again over the letter in a semi-circle

Distortion of facts

168    With angle inside the loop

Calculating mind

169   Filled up with ink

Sensuality

170    Drawn as a garland with a loop

Thoughtless, casual, friendly

171 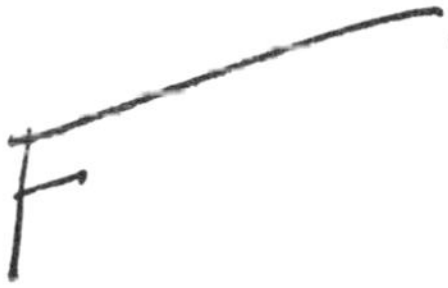   Top stroke extended over whole word

Protection, patronizing

172    With wavy lines

Sense of fun

173    Stroke going back in 8 form

Frequent in writings of female homosexuals

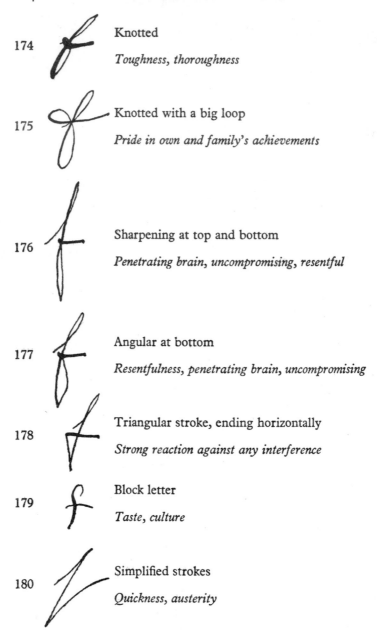

174 Knotted

Toughness, thoroughness

175 Knotted with a big loop

Pride in own and family's achievements

176 Sharpening at top and bottom

Penetrating brain, uncompromising, resentful

177 Angular at bottom

Resentfulness, penetrating brain, uncompromising

178 Triangular stroke, ending horizontally

Strong reaction against any interference

179 Block letter

Taste, culture

180 Simplified strokes

Quickness, austerity

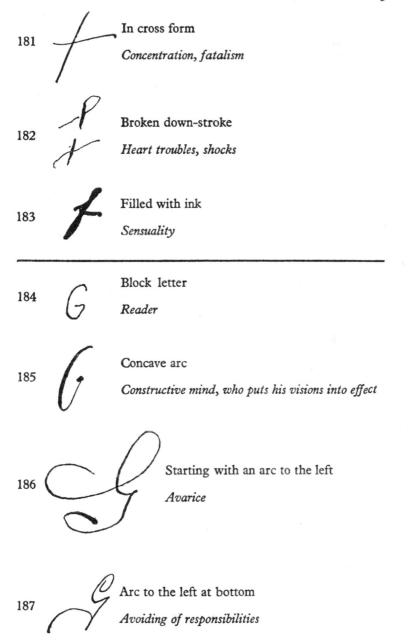

181 In cross form

Concentration, fatalism

182 Broken down-stroke

Heart troubles, shocks

183 Filled with ink

Sensuality

184 Block letter

Reader

185 Concave arc

Constructive mind, who puts his visions into effect

186 Starting with an arc to the left

Avarice

187 Arc to the left at bottom

Avoiding of responsibilities

188

Large loop at top

Muddlehead

189

Peculiar shape

Exaggerated sex imagination, lowered resistance to sex excesses and perversions

190

Two loops at the bottom

Special degree of vanity, peculiar habits and sentiments

191

Triangular, horizontally closed

Domestic tyranny, often caused by sex disappointment

192

Open and enrolled loop

No erotic fixation, in male handwritings often indicative of sexual abnormalities, especially impotence.

193

Arcade at bottom

Avoiding any sexual responsibility

194
a, b

Wide, open to the left

Contemplation, open for sensual impressions but no erotic fixation, poetic attitude to the sensual world.

195
a,b,c

Underlengths not crossed

No sexual fixation, virginity, masturbation

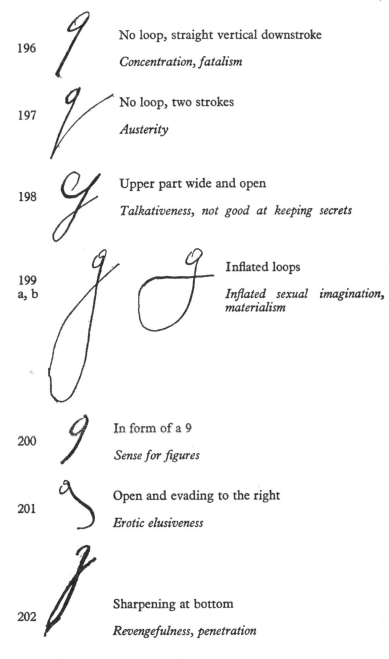

196 No loop, straight vertical downstroke

Concentration, fatalism

197 No loop, two strokes

Austerity

198 Upper part wide and open

Talkativeness, not good at keeping secrets

199
a, b

Inflated loops

Inflated sexual imagination, materialism

200 In form of a 9

Sense for figures

201 Open and evading to the right

Erotic elusiveness

202 Sharpening at bottom

Revengefulness, penetration

203   Open and nicked

Weakness, timidity

204   Triangular, with horizontal bottom

Needs solid material basis

205
a, b   Open and enrolled

No erotic fixation, insincere in sexual matters, impotence

206   End stroke going down

Vanity

207   Arc to the right

Constructive mind, who puts his visions into effect

208   Underlengths in the form of an open 8

Very frequent in writings of female homosexuals

209   Enrolled to the left

Greed, egoism

210 Narrow

Shyness

211 Stroke underlining the word

Self-admiration

212 Tasteless elaboration with vertical
stroke between

Impudence, arrogant vulgarity

213 Down stroke going under the line to the left

*Unwilling to talk things over and compromise,
believes in fighting things out*

214 Enrolled

Egoism

215 Block letter

Culture, taste

216 Amendments

Hypochondriac, self-torturing

217 Peculiar shape

*Exaggerated sex imagination, lowered resistance to
sexual excesses and perversions*

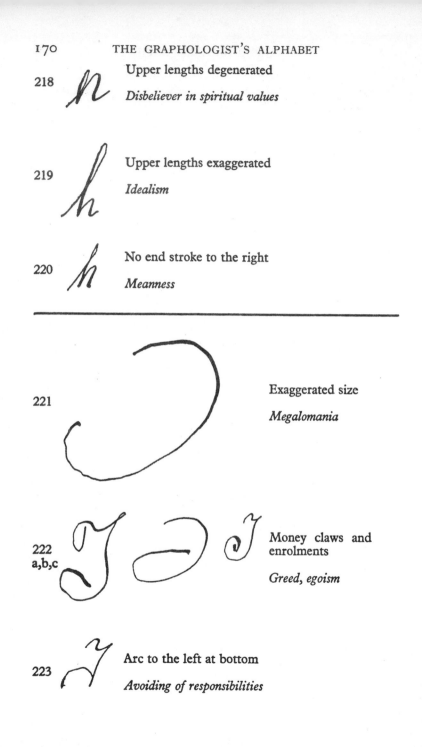

218 Upper lengths degenerated

Disbeliever in spiritual values

219 Upper lengths exaggerated

Idealism

220 No end stroke to the right

Meanness

221 Exaggerated size

Megalomania

222
a,b,c Money claws and enrolments

Greed, egoism

223 Arc to the left at bottom

Avoiding of responsibilities

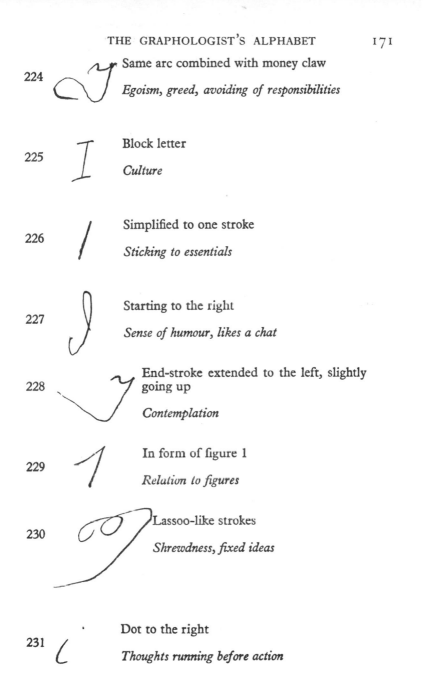

224 Same arc combined with money claw

Egoism, greed, avoiding of responsibilities

225 Block letter

Culture

226 Simplified to one stroke

Sticking to essentials

227 Starting to the right

Sense of humour, likes a chat

228 End-stroke extended to the left, slightly going up

Contemplation

229 In form of figure 1

Relation to figures

230 Lassoo-like strokes

Shrewdness, fixed ideas

231 Dot to the right

Thoughts running before action

232

Dot to the left

Caution, procrastination

233

Accurate pointing

Accuracy

234

High-flying dots

High-flying thoughts, lack of realism

235

Pointing accurately and very low

Ability for detailed work

236

Dot low and heavy

Materialism, sometimes depression

237
a,b,c

Dot in stroke or arcade form

Concealment, diplomacy, deceit

238

In accent form

Critical, discriminating mind, emphasis on principles

239   **Weak dot**

Lack of energy and vitality

240   **Dot missing**

Laziness, weakness or carelessness

241   **Little arc open to the left (watching eye)**

Good observer

242   **Dot in form of a small circle**

Inability to face facts, eccentric, crank

243   **Arc to the left**

Neurotic

244   **Dot connected with previous or following letters**

Clever combination of thoughts, ability for scientific work

245   **Enriched starting stroke**

Cumbersome and fussy

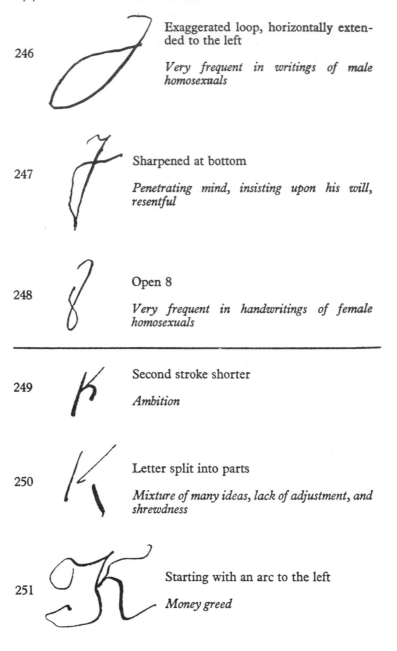

246 Exaggerated loop, horizontally extended to the left

Very frequent in writings of male homosexuals

247 Sharpened at bottom

Penetrating mind, insisting upon his will, resentful

248 Open 8

Very frequent in handwritings of female homosexuals

---

249 Second stroke shorter

Ambition

250 Letter split into parts

Mixture of many ideas, lack of adjustment, and shrewdness

251 Starting with an arc to the left

Money greed

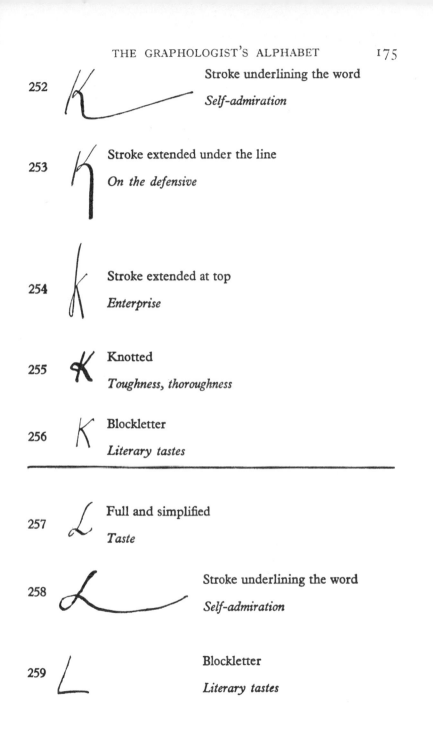

252 Stroke underlining the word

Self-admiration

253 Stroke extended under the line

On the defensive

254 Stroke extended at top

Enterprise

255 Knotted

Toughness, thoroughness

256 Blockletter

Literary tastes

257 Full and simplified

Taste

258 Stroke underlining the word

Self-admiration

259 Blockletter

Literary tastes

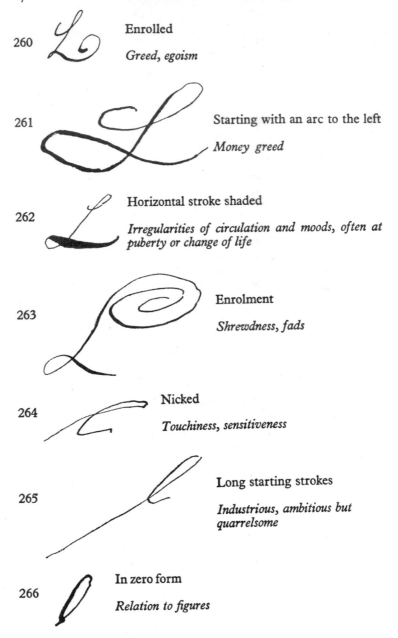

260 **Enrolled**
Greed, egoism

261 Starting with an arc to the left
Money greed

262 Horizontal stroke shaded
Irregularities of circulation and moods, often at puberty or change of life

263 Enrolment
Shrewdness, fads

264 Nicked
Touchiness, sensitiveness

265 Long starting strokes
Industrious, ambitious but quarrelsome

266 In zero form
Relation to figures

267  Down-stroke broken

Heart troubles, shocks

268  Amended

Hypochondria

269  Sharpening top and bottom

Insists on getting his own way, penetrating brain, resentful

270  Capital *M* mounting

Ambitious, but dependent on public opinion and acknowledgement

271  Capital *M* descending

Aristocratic feeling, condescension, pride

272  Starting with an arc far under the line

Actor, poser, orator

273  Square

Technical skill

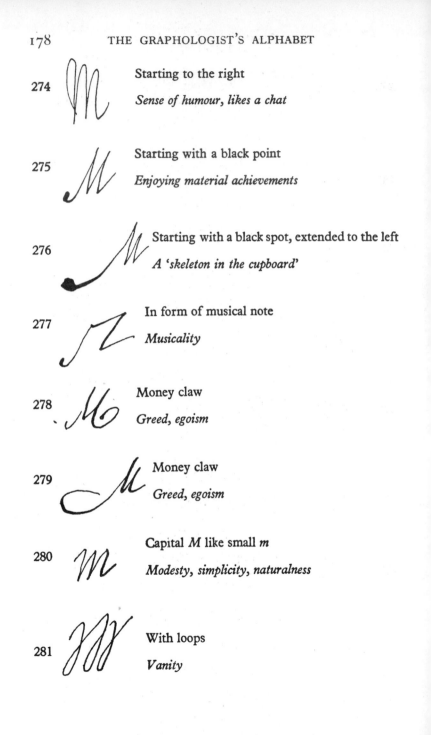

274   Starting to the right

Sense of humour, likes a chat

275   Starting with a black point

Enjoying material achievements

276   Starting with a black spot, extended to the left

A 'skeleton in the cupboard'

277   In form of musical note

Musicality

278   Money claw

Greed, egoism

279   Money claw

Greed, egoism

280   Capital *M* like small *m*

Modesty, simplicity, naturalness

281   With loops

Vanity

282   **Middle part of three parts lower**

More dependent upon public than on individual opinion

283   **Middle part of three parts higher**

More dependent on private than on public opinion

284   **Full and round**

Imagination

285   **End-stroke going back and crossing the letter**

If in signature, suicide tendencies

286   **Garland**

Kindness, friendliness

287   **So-called *sacré cœur*, taught in some Catholic convents**

Aristocratic pretensions

288   **Arcade form**

Diplomacy, impenetrability

289    **Wavy line**

Versatility

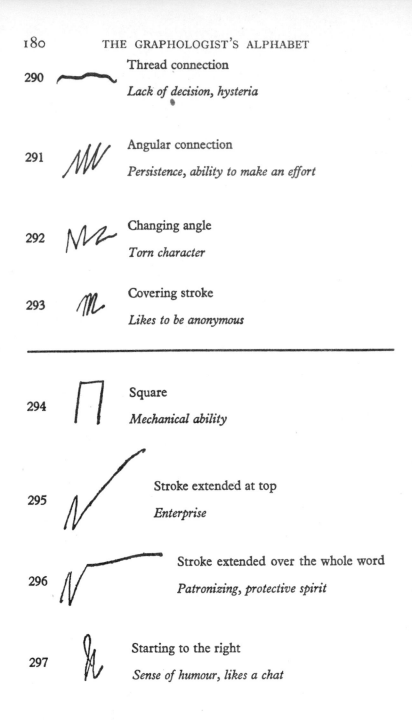

290 Thread connection

Lack of decision, hysteria

291 Angular connection

Persistence, ability to make an effort

292 Changing angle

Torn character

293 Covering stroke

Likes to be anonymous

294 Square

Mechanical ability

295 Stroke extended at top

Enterprise

296 Stroke extended over the whole word

Patronizing, protective spirit

297 Starting to the right

Sense of humour, likes a chat

298   End-stroke extending under the line and left

Prefers fighting things out instead of compromise

298a   Block letter going over into a wavy line

Versatility within the limits of firm, traditional habits

---

299   Enclosed

Secretiveness

300   Open

Sincerity

301   Peculiar shape

Exaggerated sex imagination, with lowered resistance against sexual excesses and perversions

302   In zero form

Relation to figures

303   Starting with an arc

Sense of humour, likes a chat

304   Open at bottom

Hypocrisy

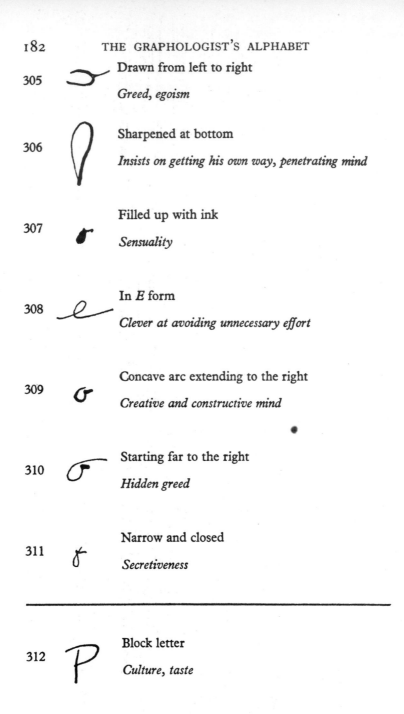

305 Drawn from left to right

Greed, egoism

306 Sharpened at bottom

Insists on getting his own way, penetrating mind

307 Filled up with ink

Sensuality

308 In *E* form

Clever at avoiding unnecessary effort

309 Concave arc extending to the right

Creative and constructive mind

310 Starting far to the right

Hidden greed

311 Narrow and closed

Secretiveness

312 Block letter

Culture, taste

313   Peculiar shape

Exaggerated sex imagination, with lowered resistance against sexual excesses and perversions

314   Arcs extended to the left

Vulgarity, bad taste

315
a, b   Enrolments

Shrewdness, sometimes fixed ideas

316   Slightly enrolled

Enterprise, business mind

317   Enrolment ending in a point

Enjoying material successes

318   Up- and down-stroke forking

Austerity, talkativeness

319   Curve extended to the left

Greed

320   First stroke higher

Enterprise

321		Consisting of two arcs *Constructive and creative mind*

322		Broad horizontal stroke *Vigour, brutality*

323 a, b		In form of musical notes *Musicality*

324		Block letter *Reader, culture*

325		Second down-stroke shorter *Ambition*

326		Stroke extended to the top *Enterprise*

327		Carefully shaped *Culture*

328		In form of musical notes *Musicality*

329   Rounded at top

Routine, changeability

330   Second part lower

Curiosity

331   Loops

Vanity, prejudice

332   Narrow

Exclusiveness, inhibition

333   End-stroke going up and back

Distortion of facts

---

334   Simplified

Culture, taste

335   Printed

Culture, fond of reading

336   Enlarged to the left

Vulgarity, lack of taste, greed

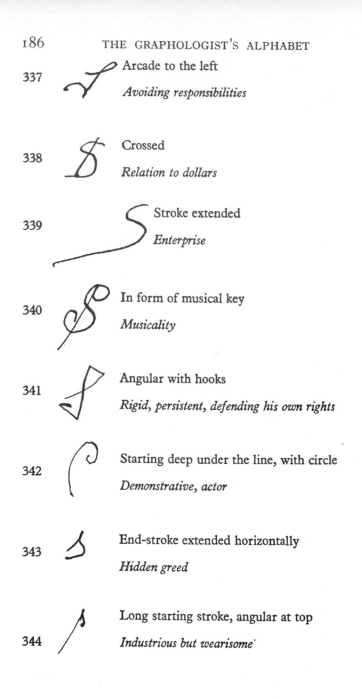

337 Arcade to the left

Avoiding responsibilities

338 Crossed

Relation to dollars

339 Stroke extended

Enterprise

340 In form of musical key

Musicality

341 Angular with hooks

Rigid, persistent, defending his own rights

342 Starting deep under the line, with circle

Demonstrative, actor

343 End-stroke extended horizontally

Hidden greed

344 Long starting stroke, angular at top

Industrious but wearisome˙

345 Grasping claw

Greed, egoism

346 Enrolled

Shrewdness

347 Closed

Secretiveness

---

348 Top stroke roofing over the whole word

Spirit of protection, patronizing

349 Arcs extended to the left

Fussiness, bad taste, vulgarity

350 Knotted

Toughness, thoroughness

351 With large loop

Pride in own achievements

352 Cross going down

Disappointed, sulky, resentful, low opinion of others

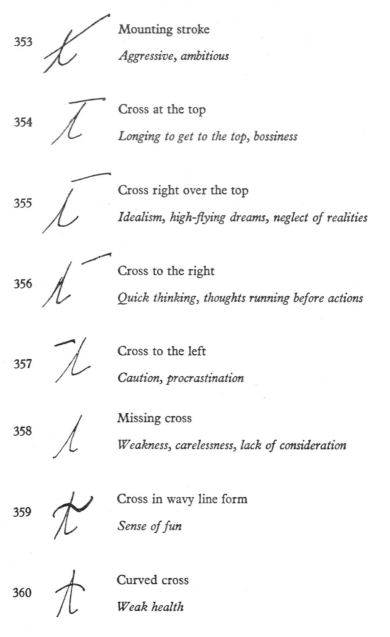

353 Mounting stroke

Aggressive, ambitious

354 Cross at the top

Longing to get to the top, bossiness

355 Cross right over the top

Idealism, high-flying dreams, neglect of realities

356 Cross to the right

Quick thinking, thoughts running before actions

357 Cross to the left

Caution, procrastination

358 Missing cross

Weakness, carelessness, lack of consideration

359 Cross in wavy line form

Sense of fun

360 Curved cross

Weak health

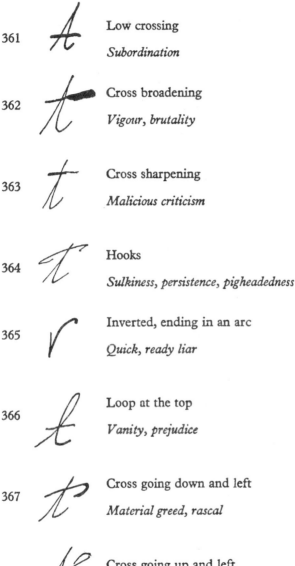

361   Low crossing

Subordination

362   Cross broadening

Vigour, brutality

363   Cross sharpening

Malicious criticism

364   Hooks

Sulkiness, persistence, pigheadedness

365   Inverted, ending in an arc

Quick, ready liar

366   Loop at the top

Vanity, prejudice

367   Cross going down and left

Material greed, rascal

368   Cross going up and left

Egoism

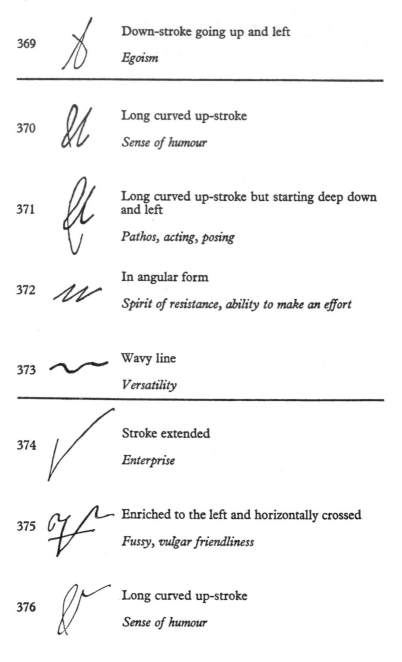

369   Down-stroke going up and left

Egoism

---

370   Long curved up-stroke

Sense of humour

371   Long curved up-stroke but starting deep down and left

Pathos, acting, posing

372   In angular form

Spirit of resistance, ability to make an effort

373   Wavy line

Versatility

---

374   Stroke extended

Enterprise

375   Enriched to the left and horizontally crossed

Fussy, vulgar friendliness

376   Long curved up-stroke

Sense of humour

377 Crossing through and left

Disappointment, in signatures suicidal tendencies

378 Simplified and angular

Clear, penetrating brain

379 Simplified and angular

Clear, penetrating brain

380 Stroke extended

Enterprise

381 Long curved up-stroke

Sense of humour

382 In peculiar form

Strong sex imagination, lowered resistance against sexual excesses and perversions

383 Enlarged to the left

Vulgarity, bad taste

384 In form of two crossing strokes

Precision, fighting spirit

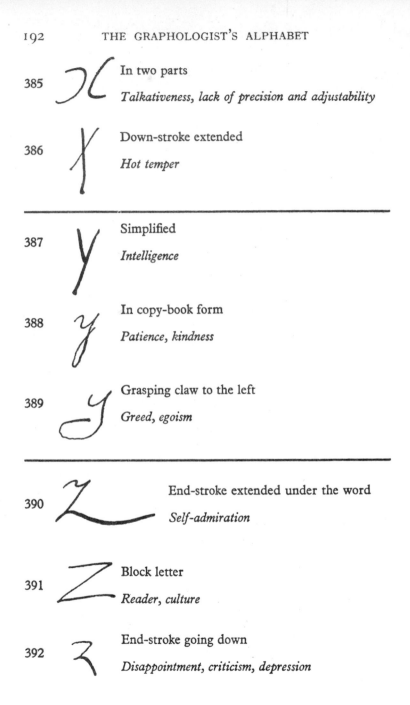

385   In two parts

Talkativeness, lack of precision and adjustability

386   Down-stroke extended

Hot temper

387   Simplified

Intelligence

388   In copy-book form

Patience, kindness

389   Grasping claw to the left

Greed, egoism

390   End-stroke extended under the word

Self-admiration

391   Block letter

Reader, culture

392   End-stroke going down

Disappointment, criticism, depression

PART THREE

GRAPHOLOGICAL EXERCISES

I. IDENTIFICATION

Quiz I

Each of the four rectangles has been drawn by one of each of the four writers of the word 'money.' Try to find out which rectangles belong to which writer, and give reasons for your decision.

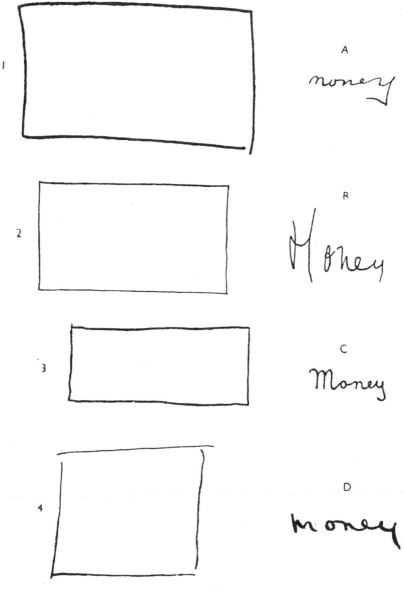

I have taken the word 'Dear' out of 24 ordinary letters and cut it in two. Find out which Ds belong to the corresponding 'ears'. Oh dear!

A

ear

B

ear

C

ear

D

ear

E

ear

F

ear

G

ear

H

ear

I

ear

J

ear

K

ear

L

ear

M

ear

N

ear

O

ear

P

ear

R

ear

S

ear

T

ear

U

ear

V

ear

X

ear

Y

ear

Z

ear

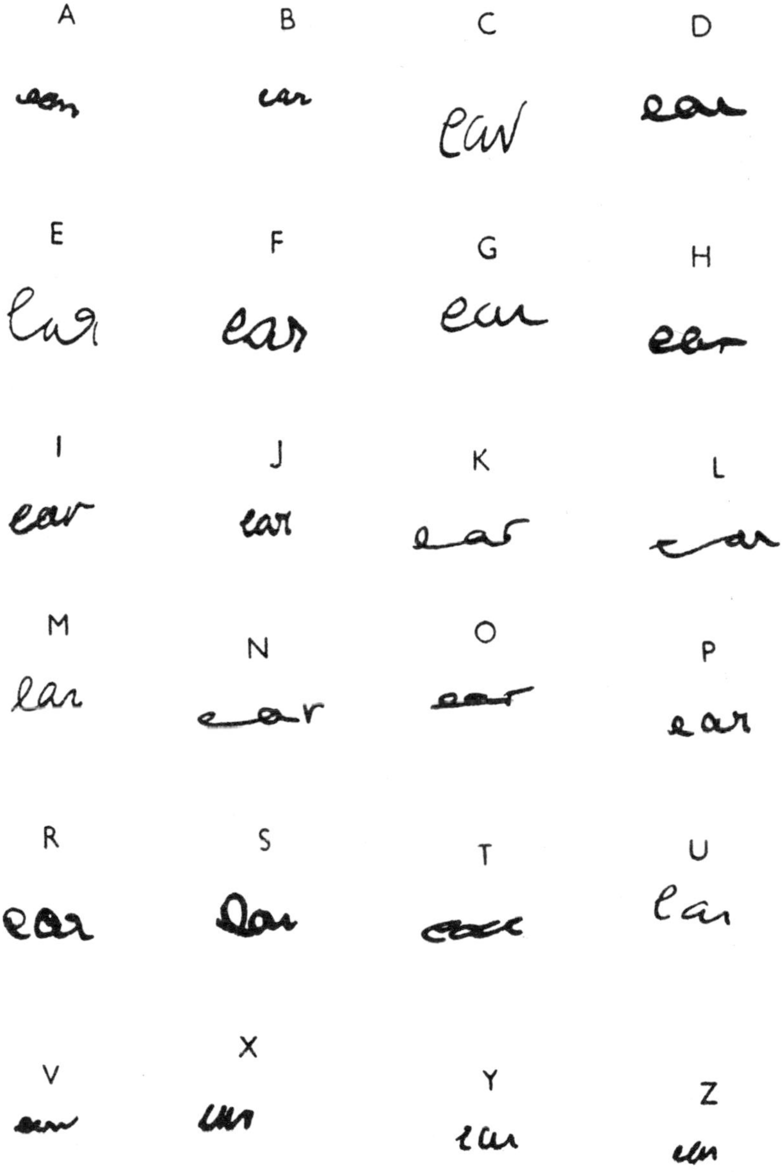

Quiz 3

Here again I took 20 ordinary letters and cut out the word 'Dear' as well as the last word of the letter—either 'yours', 'sincerely,' 'faithfully' or 'truly.' Can you find out which words are written by the same writers?

A

faithfully.

B

Faithfully

C

Faithfully

D

Yours

E

Yours

F

sincerely

G

faithfully

H

truly.

I

sincerely

J

sincerely

K

faithfully,

L

faithfully

M

sincerely

N

O

truly.

P

sincerely

Q

sincerely,

R

faithfully

S

sincerely

T

faithfully,

Quiz 4

Even figures are written in the same characteristic way as letters. I took 19 envelopes addressed to myself and cut the figures 29 away from Abercorn Place. Put together the ones which belong together.

1	2	3	4	5	6
29	29	29,	29,	29	29,

7	8	9	10	11	12
29,	29	29.	29	29	29

13	14	15	16	17	18	19
29	29	29	29	29	29,	29.

A — Abercorn Place,

B — Abercorn Place

C — ABERCORN PLACE

D — Abercorn Place

E — Abercorn Place

F — Abercorn Place,

G — Abercorn Place.

H — Abercorn Place

I — Abercorn Place,

J — Abercorn Place

K — Abercorn Place

L — Abercorn Place

M — Abercorn Place,

N — Abercorn Place

O — Abercorn Place

P — Abercorn Place

Q — Abercorne Rd

R — Abercorn Place,

S — Abercorn Place

Quiz 5

Among the writing examples on this page there are two by the same writer, one written with his right, the other with his left hand. Find out which ones they are and give reasons.

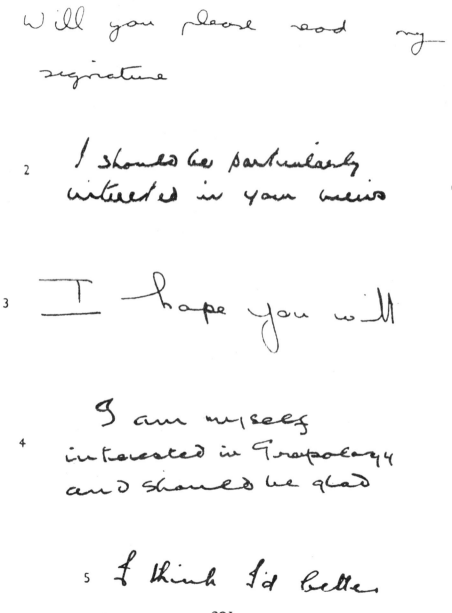

Will you please read my signature

2 I should be particularly interested in your views

3 I hope you will

4 I am myself interested in Graphology and should be glad

5 I think I'd better

Quiz 6

It is agreed among graphologists that sex and age cannot be assessed from handwriting. The reason is that mentally we all have qualities of both sexes and that the calendar age does not necessarily correspond to the physical and mental strength and vitality of a particular writer.

Laymen often refuse to believe that while graphology can assess the most subtle types of character it fails over such obvious matters ; and they claim that even a layman can assess whether a particular letter comes from a man or a woman, and what the age of the writer is.

I have put together, just as they came and with no special choice of particularly strong or weak people, extracts from different letters. Try to find out the sex and the age of the writers. You will be surprised how often you are wrong.

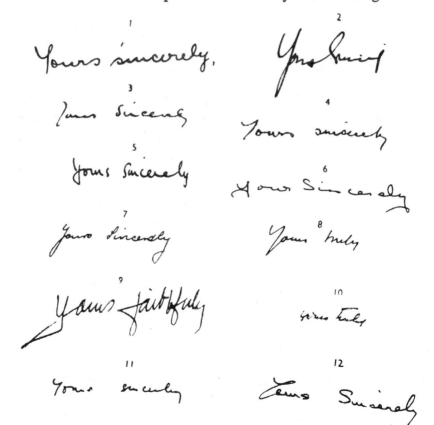

Yours sincerely [13]

Yours Truly [14]

[signature] [15]

Yours faithfully [16]

Quiz 7

Here are three sentences written by three different writers twice, once at their normal and once at their maximum speed. Find out which is the quick and which is the normal writing, and give reasons for your decision.

1 Love to all friends in New York

2 Love to all my friends in New York.

3 I will give this

4 I will give this

5 I have got a cold

6 I have got a cold

Here is an example of disguised writing in its most frequent, but in some ways most difficult form, namely, printed in block letters (Example 1). The normal writing of the writer is among the other examples. Find out which one it is.

1 *I doubt if you can guess who I am*

2 *Would you please*

3 *This is my condition*

4 *Yours Sincerely*

5 *Thanking you,*

Quiz 9

Here is another form of disguise: mirror writing (Example 1). Who among the writers of the other examples, which are in natural style, wrote it?

1   *Airtw llē tannas l*

2   *addressed envelope*

3   *Handwriting in the following*

4   *Yours faithfully*

5   *so will end.*

This is one of the most difficult quizzes in the book. The same sentence is written fifteen times. Find out by how many different writers it is written, and state which examples are written by the same writer.

1 The quick brown fox jumps over the lazy dog.

2 The quick brown fox jumps over the lazy dog.

3 The quick brown fox jumps over the lazy dog.

4 The quick brown fox jumps over the lazy dog.

5 The quick brown fox jumps over the lazy dog.

6 The quick brown fox jumps over the lazy dog.

7 The quick brown fox jumps over the lazy dog.

8 The quick brown fox jumps over the lazy dog

9 The quick brown fox jumps over the lazy dog

10 The quick brown fox jumps over the lazy dog

11 The quick brown fox jumps over the lazy dog

12 The quick brown fox jumps over the lazy dog

13 The quick brown fox jumps over the lazy dog

14 The quick brown fox jumps over the lazy dog.

15 The quick brown fox jumps over the lazy dog.

Quiz 11

Another example of disguised writing, this time in a stylised handwriting (Example 1). Which of the writers of the other examples wrote it?

1 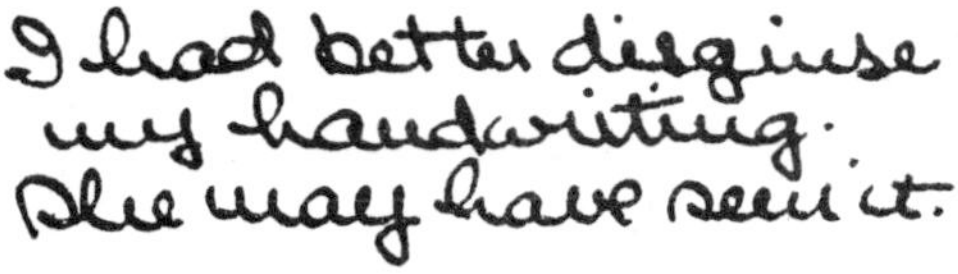
I had better disguise
my handwriting.
She may have seen it.

2 
Would you please

3 

4 
He says that it is

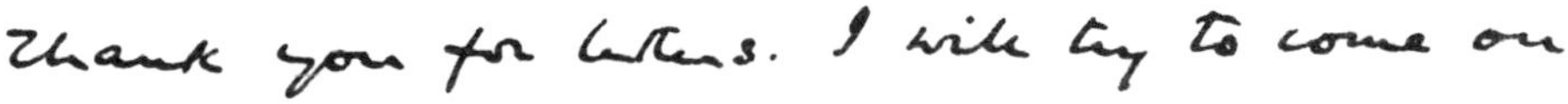
Thank you for letters. I will try to come on

6 
I should be very grateful

7 
I can only write

Are the examples 1 to 6 written by the same person or by different persons? If you think by different persons, are any of them written by the same person, or are they all different?

1   so clever a turn

2   What still in tears?

3   You are more worthless and than millions like this

4   up and Acid formed

5   occur, both the old & the

6   My Dear Dr. Singer

Quiz 13

All these four examples are written by the same lady at different ages; one when she was 13, one when she was 20, one when she was 26, and one when she was 39.

State which is which.

I have noticed a certain parallel between the Finns & the Irish, a parallel which first came to me as I listened to some of the F. folk songs.

2   *4) outfit more expensive —
Cabinet, drawers
5) at present less familiar to readers.*

3   *Went to Stockbury in the morning. Lovely day*

4   *The problem is — where is to house these fantastic trophies as each one seems*

And what about these two examples?
Are they written by the same person?

1

2

Now we come to forgeries. Example 1 is an original signature.
Find out whether the other examples are originals or forgeries.

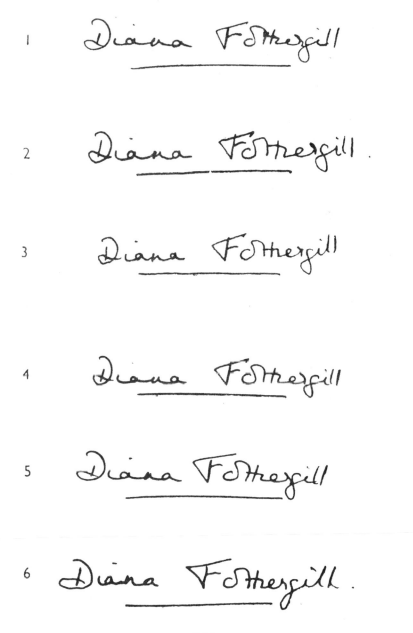

Example A is an original. The two others are forged, but one is imitated and the other one is traced. Find out which is which.

A

B

C

Example A is original writing. Are the other examples forgeries and, if not, which ones are not?

A   *fine Pounds,*

B   *fine Pounds*

C   *fine Pounds*

D   *fine hundred Pounds*

E   *fifty fine Pounds*

F   *fine hundred Pounds*

II. ANALYSIS

   Give a short character portrait of this Englishwoman in her thirties.

Dear Dr. Singer,
   After only two articles on the subject of Graphology, which I have read with great interest, I am writing to ask you whether you would be so kind as to give me a reading. (Stamped addressed envelope enclosed).
   You may use this letter as an example if you care to as long as my identity is not disclosed.

Quiz 19

Give a short character portrait of this young lady who learned to write on the continent of Europe.

wish to do so   As regards the scrawl on
this page you   may use it if you think fit

Quiz 20

Give a short character description of this Englishman.

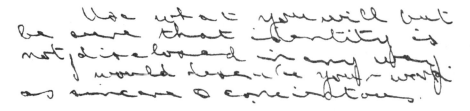

(Reproduced approximately half-size of original)

Quiz 21

Give a short character portrait of this Englishman.

In conclusion, I dont mind you making use of my handwriting as a specimen for comment in any of your future articles but I would like my name and address to be treated in Confidence.

III. APPLICATIONS OF GRAPHOLOGY

Quiz 22

In January, 1949, a man came to a bank in Bristol and asked for the manager. The manager was not there and the man left a note for him, which you see here.

He came again half an hour later, shot the manager and robbed the bank. He was never caught alive. But the police file on the subject is now closed.

After the murder, I was interviewed by an evening paper about the unknown man.

What would you have said about him after examining the writing?

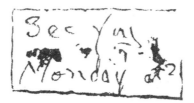

Quiz 23

This is the signature of C. C. Kennedy, an Oxford graduate and former employee of an accountants' firm, also an amateur motor racer.. He tried to rob a bank in Northumberland in September, 1949, killed two people, and when surrounded by police shot himself.

Compare his writing with the writing of the Bristol bank murderer. Do you find any similarities between the two?

Suppose these are letters applying for a job. Pick a good secretary from among these applicants.

1

Sir

I wish to apply for the post

2

my nomination of that

3

we are came

4

tell me so.

5

May I apply for

6

Dear Sir

With reference to your letter

Pick a good commercial traveller from among these applicants.

1

I would like to know

2.

Please forward

3.

order which I should be

4

Would you kindly

5

Dear Sir,

Quiz 26

Great excitement in the house of Dr. Smith and his family. For the first time after the war they have the chance of getting a housemaid. They badly wanted domestic help.

Three applicants have written from Germany for the job. A responsible person is needed as there is much valuable property in the house. There are also some small children who need patience and care.

It is difficult to pick the right person, as reliable references are not available.

Which one would you choose?

1

Herrn Doktor,

2

einen
ja prima
schwarzer. Ich weiss
feld ver hältnisse sind.

3

also Kate

Quiz 27

Where do they come from?

National types of writing are different.

In which part of the world would you say these four writers were born and bred?

1

2 Museum 57

3 Sydney Nova Scotia

4 Queen Juliana

Quiz 28

Signatures are sometimes revealing about a person's profession, either actual or potential, or about his or her hobbies and inclinations.

What can you say about each of these seven examples?

Graphologists cannot yet make a correct diagnosis of a particular illness by handwriting, although our findings often support the doctor and always the psychiatrist.

But we can say whether writing looks healthy to us, or whether either physical health, or nervous balance, seems to have been weakened.

What would you think of these five examples?

1   *please*

2   *London.*

3   *would you*

4

5   *London*

Suppose your old landlady comes to you in despair. One of her lodgers has been missing for two days and a slip on his desk seems to indicate an intention to take his life.

"He was a very serious and reliable young man, somewhere from the Continent." She has no complaints.

But not all her lodgers have been like him and the good old lady has several times in her long life been the victim of crude practical jokes.

She is therefore reluctant to go to the police and she asks you what you think of this writing:

Is there an indication, a real danger of suicide, or may it turn out to be a practical joke again?

Is there a change in handwriting when character and social standards change?

Here are two signatures by Benito Mussolini, before and after he came to power.

What changes can you note?

Quiz 32

Parents are legitimately concerned about their children's choice when they contemplate marriage.

In the case of the Hopspoons, this concern was particularly justifiable as Ronald was their only son, young and inexperienced, and had met the girl after the war in Germany, where his parents had no chance to inspect her.

Suppose they came to you and asked your opinion about her writing. What would you say?

femme in 3 Tagen

Quiz 33

There are two writings on this page, the upper one by a gentleman, the lower one by a lady.

If you were asked whether you think this couple would make a good match in marriage, what would you say?

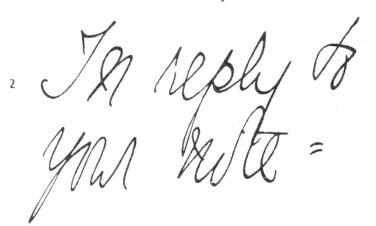

Quiz 34

Is this writer generous, normal, or mean?

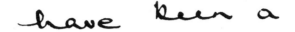

Quiz 35

Can you learn anything from doodles? If so, what does this one tell you?

Quiz 36

These are scribbles of two children about four. Do they tell you something about their characters?

1

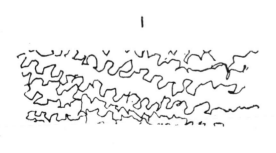

2

Look at this set of drawings and doodles and try and give an assessment of the author. They are all by the same hand.

Quiz 38

These are written by children aged between 9 and 10. Do you think they are just average, normal children, or is something wrong with one or other of them?

1. *London*

2. (daddy)

3. I dont lice riting

Quiz 39

Which of these three children of the same school form is the most healthy and intelligent?

1. two Easter eggs.

2. We have Easter

3. Easter eggs are

Quiz 40

What was in the mind of the man who drew this doodle?

Quiz 41

Here are two signatures of Adolf Hitler, the first before, the second after his rise to power. What do they reveal?

IV. ANSWERS

Quiz 1

No. 1 has been drawn by writer D, easily recognisable by the strong pressure of the stroke and the slight slant to the left of the vertical stroke.

No. 2 has been drawn by writer C. Both are very regular and completely upright.

No. 3 has been drawn by writer B. Both are upright. In both the stroke is extended at the top.

No. 4 is drawn by writer A. Both are done a bit haphazardly. Both are slightly inclined to the right.

Quiz 2

1 belongs to O	13 belongs to J
2 belongs to V	14 belongs to E
3 belongs to G	15 belongs to N
4 belongs to A	16 belongs to K
5 belongs to U	17 belongs to P
6 belongs to B	18 belongs to F
7 belongs to N	19 belongs to L
8 belongs to H	20 belongs to R
9 belongs to C	21 belongs to X
10 belongs to T	22 belongs to S
11 belongs to D	23 belongs to Z
12 belongs to I	24 belongs to Y

If you do not believe me, cut them out and put them together.

Quiz 3

1 belongs to G	6 belongs to B
2 belongs to J	7 belongs to H
3 belongs to A	8 belongs to C
4 belongs to K	9 belongs to D
5 belongs to I	10 belongs to E

11 belongs to L	16 belongs to N
12 belongs to F	17 belongs to R
13 belongs to M	18 belongs to O
14 belongs to Q	19 belongs to P
15 belongs to T	20 belongs to S

Quiz 4

1 belongs to M	11 belongs to L
2 belongs to J	12 belongs to I
3 belongs to B	13 belongs to O
4 belongs to F	14 belongs to P
5 belongs to E	15 belongs to R
6 belongs to G	16 belongs to S
7 belongs to A	17 belongs to Q
8 belongs to C	18 belongs to N
9 belongs to D	19 belongs to K
10 belongs to H	

Quiz 5

Examples 2 and 4 come from the same writer. The first is written with his right, the second with his left hand. Left-hand writing often slants to the left. The left-hand writing is also broader.

But the shaping of letters, proportion, extension to top and bottom are almost identical and the form and degree of connection show almost no alteration. (See the words 'interested in'.)

Quiz 6

Writing No. 1 belongs to a gentleman aged 50, No. 2 to a lady aged 50, No. 3 to a lady aged over 60, No. 4 to a lady aged 38, No. 5 to a lady aged 28, No. 6 to a lady aged 19, No. 7 to a lady aged 19, No. 8 to a gentleman aged 33, No. 9 to a gentleman aged 35, No. 10 to a lady aged 68, No. 11 to a lady aged 25, No. 12 to a lady aged 47, No. 13 to a lady aged 65, No. 14 to a lady in her late fifties, No. 15 to a gentleman over 65, and No. 16 to a lady aged 40.

Quiz 7

No. 1 is the quick, No. 2 is the normal writing. No. 1 is broader. The word 'to,' the letter 'r' in York are left out. There is no full stop after York. There are only two breaks inside words, while in No. 2 there are seven.

No. 3 is the quick, No. 4 the normal writing. This is more difficult to assess, because the normal writing of this writer is already very quick. But writing No. 3 is broader, letters are more simplified, the *t* cross in the word 'this' is farther to the right and crosses in fact the *h* only without touching the *t*. The *i* dot in 'this' again is completely left out.

No. 5 is the normal, No. 6 is the quick writing. No. 6 is much broader, less regular, more inclined to the right, and the end strokes (see the word 'cold') are more extended.

Quiz 8

Example No. 1 has been done by the writer of Example No. 3. Note the identical type of stroke, soft, pasty and colourful, as if it had been drawn with a fine brush and not written with a pen. Note also the mounting *t* crosses in both writings, the little loops of the *d* in 'doubt' (Example 1), of the *s* in 'is' and of the *t* in 'condition' (Example 3). Note the turns to the left: the *Y,y* and *g* in Example 1, and *d* in Example 3. Note the identical proportions and the characteristic forming of the letter *m* with the first two downstrokes close and the third further apart (*m* in Example 1, *my* in Example 3).

Quiz 9

Example 1 was written by the writer of Example 3. He alone shows the same light hand and light pressure, and the roundness of connection and fullness which is seen in Example 1.

Quiz 10

All examples with the exception of Example No. 10 are written by the same person. They all, though expertly written in different styles with much variety, show a very straight and regular bottom line and very clear shaping of the individual letters. The round strokes are all carefully rounded.

This is different in Example 10. The line jumps several times up and down. The letter *o* (brown, fox, over) is hardly rounded, but slightly angular at bottom. The *c* in 'quick' and the *z* in 'lazy' are straight down strokes without any attempt to give them a round shape. Compare also the down stroke of the *k* in 'quick' which in all other writings is clearly drawn to the bottom of the line, while in Example 10 it is horizontally extended above the line. The *t* cross in 'the' is horizontal in all other examples, but rising in Example 10.

Quiz 11

The writer of the disguised writing of Example 1 is the writer of Example 5. It is the maturity and culture of the writing and the pressure and shading of the stroke which gives her away. Proportion, regularity, broadness are the same in Examples 1 and 5. So is the degree of flow and connection and the round open garland-like form of connection.

The concurrent tasteful simplicity and fullness of the writing, the correct placing and identical character and distance of *i* dots and full stops, the horizontal crossing of the *t* and *f* letters, the almost identical shaping of the first *s* in 'disguised' (Example 1) and in 'letters' (Example 5) are further indications. So is the closing and sometimes knotting of the *a* and *o* letters.

Quiz 12

All examples are written by the same gentleman, but at different ages.

He was 15 when he wrote Example 1, 18 when writing Example 2, 21 when writing Example 3, 30 when writing Example 4, 34 when writing Example 5, and 41 when writing Example 6.

The general character of the writing has changed little, but Examples 1 and 2 are written more slowly and according to text-book. Examples 3 and 4 more vigorously and less convention-ally, while in Examples 5 and 6 he has already found his personal style of combining traditional forms with individual taste.

Quiz 13

Example 3 was written when the writer was 13, Example 2 when she was 20, Example 1 when she was 26, and Example 4 when she was 39. She married between the ages of 20 and 26, and had a child between the ages of 26 and 39.

Examples 1 and 2 are still written in an orthodox way, stiff and a bit cramped.

Example 1 shows already a natural and easy flow, still more Example 4 which is also broader.

Quiz 14

These two writings look very similar. But there are small differences in the forming of the figure *3* and in the letters *H, f* and *d*. Writing 1 shows greater pressure, more loops, less extension to the left (*3* and *S* in Example 2), different end strokes of words and thicker, rising horizontal strokes.

They are written by two different persons. But these are identical (uniovular) twin brothers, which explains the similarity.

Quiz 15

Apart from Example 1, Examples 4 and 5 are originals, the rest are imitations.

Compare the natural and genuine flow of the originals with the slow and trembling features of the forgeries. The loop of the *D* in 'Diana' is especially interesting for comparison.

Quiz 16

Example B is imitated. Example C is traced. The size and the width of the word and the distance of the underlining stroke from it, discloses that B could not have been traced. On the other hand B looks a bit more natural, while C is too much a copy of A.

Quiz 17

All the Examples B to F are forgeries. But C is traced, while the others are imitations.

B, D, E and F are very shakily written much slower than the original, more trembling, and the stroke looks different under the magnifying glass. It is more indented and uneven.

The traced Example C looks very similar to the original but the pressure is lighter. The whole thing looks more like a hand-struck stamp than handwriting.

Quiz 18

The writer is an intelligent and imaginative person. (Arrangement, fullness of writing.)

She is very friendly, kind and well-mannered. She is rather generous and shows a nice sense of humour. (Roundness of writing.)

She is neither outstandingly quick nor slow. Her brain works smoothly and she is well able to solve problems. (Connected writing.) She is good at figures and used to dealing with them. (Figure writing.) She is business-minded and sees her advantage.

She is rather talkative, likes to travel and to get around. (Broad writing.) She has good taste and is very neat and tidy. (Neat writing.) She also keeps good relations with her mirror. (Loops.)

She is very disciplined (regular writing), versatile and an excellent diplomatist (wavy line connection).

She tries to get her way rather by clever diplomacy than by pushing and forcing decisions. (Round writing, light pressure.) A consoling white lie seems to her the lesser evil compared to the brutal truth.

She generally dislikes everything which is too forceful, too loud, too alarming, too sensual, too glaring or too shrill. Her ideal is rather a life in water colours. (Soft, but colourful shading of the strokes, light pressure.)

This is also decisive for her relation to sex. Although it plays its part in her imagination and life (downstrokes of *y* and *g* letters), she regards it as something rather troublesome and keeps it under control (regularity).

Quiz 19

The writer is a very intelligent and clear-minded person with a good education. (Simplification of writing, spacing.)

She is imaginative, a keen reader and student. She shows many interests and a desire always to know more, and also to find out about herself. She is also extremely musical. (Form of letters, some musical notes.)

She is a good observer, very intuitive and analytical. (Disconnected writing.) She is used to accurate detail work, shows tidiness and great manual dexterity. (Accurate dotting of *i*'s.) She is realistic, topical and thorough. (Size and proportion of writing.)

She has a quick wit and the power to simplify issues and to reduce them to the necessary essentials. But as she has to cope with many ideas and interests she finds it at times difficult to adjust herself to all of them and this may sometimes affect her memory. (Disconnected writing.) But she is disciplined and clever in husbanding her energies, which are not of the forceful and overwhelming type. She has a good technique of concentration, as far as her memory and her many interests and talents allow. (Straight downstrokes.)

Socially she is very well-mannered, kind and friendly. (Margins, spacing, roundness.) She is free of self-dramatization and any form of showing off or bossiness (small writing), but she is very discriminating (spacing), sometimes critical and occasionally argumentative (some rising *t* crosses).

She is basically a good mixer, active and enthusiastic (slant to the right), but in her strong discrimination lies an element of isolation.

She shows normal and at times strong sexual desires. (Extension of down strokes.)

Quiz 20

The writer is a quick, clever and imaginative person (quick, full writing). He adores open spaces, travelling and good talk, and would not be happy if compelled to live and work in a confined place (broad writing).

He is business-minded, quite good at figures (some letters written like figures) and he likes to put things on a sound material basis (extension of downstrokes).

He has his own particular tastes and likes things to be a bit different and out of the way (shaping of letters).

He likes to simplify issues (simplified writing) but is accurate about details (correct dotting of the i).

He is friendly and rather generous (broad round writing, extended end strokes).

He does not like making decisions and although he has to make them in the end, it always puts a certain nervous strain on him when he comes face to face with them (thread connection).

Here is one of the main sources of difficulty for him: while he is in fact very suggestible and spontaneous, there is always a second voice in him, restraining him from coming out of his shell completely and from behaving as enthusiastically and naturally as he really wants to, and is able to (back slant). It also prevents him recognising that he could break all the links with his past and early experiences if he wished.

His other difficulty is sex. He has, as in all things, his own tastes, and his imagination is so strongly inflated that no satisfaction completely fulfils his sexual aspirations (exaggerated extension to the bottom with inflated loops).

In this way sex is at the same time a source of constant inspiration, but also of constant irritation to him.

Quiz 21

The writing shows clear-mindedness (clear writing) and discipline (regular writing).

The writer is able to express himself well (clear shaping and spacing of words) and likes conversation (broad writing).

He is friendly (round writing), but likes an argument (rising *t* crosses).

He is accurate (correct dotting of the i's), thorough (extension to the bottom), and tidy (neat writing).

Quiz 22

The simplification of the writing and the shaping of the letters shows that the writer belongs to the educated classes. It also shows manual skill and accuracy.

The letter *S*, drawn like the figure 5, shows that he is used to dealing with figures. The spacing between words reveals that in normal circumstances he is socially discriminating. The square *M* shows mechanical skill, and the speed of the writing quickness.

The up and downs of the line show his highly emotional character. The smudgy and dotted writing indicates a high degree of sensuality, great inner tension and dependence on instincts, sometimes (see the *t*) brutal instincts.

The knotting of the *o* and the covering stroke of the *d* show secretiveness.

The changing angle shows his excitable nature and his tendency to a double life. The long weak downstrokes indicate his preoccupation with the lower elements in his own nature, also suicidal tendencies.

The sharpening of the end strokes of the words reveals cruelty. The broadness of the writing shows desire for adventure.

Quiz 23

Both writings are upright with occasional slant to the right. The proportion between large and small letters is almost the same (note the *d*). Parts of letters are left out in both writings (*u* in 'you,' second *n* in 'Kennedy').

Of the two *e*'s in 'see,' the second is smaller and higher on the line. This applies also to the two *C*'s in C. C. Kennedy.

The shaping of similar letters like *n*, *e* and *d*, although unconnected in the first disguised and printed writing, shows great similarity.

The line rises initially and then droops in both writings.

The distance between down strokes and the space between words is almost identical.

The second part of the *o* in 'you' and the first part of the *y* in 'Kennedy' show exactly the same shape and angle.

Quiz 24

There are many intelligent and gifted people amongst these writers. It depends, of course, what qualities are wanted in the particular job.

If it is speed, Example 5 would be the favourite.

But in general I would think Example 4 is the most suitable candidate.

The writing is clear, neat, intelligently simplified and well spaced. These are indications of clear-mindedness, discrimination, tidiness, and the ability to express himself.

The regularity of the writing is a sign of discipline.

Good health and vitality are shown in the degree of pressure. The colourfulness of the stroke reveals imagination.

The low *t* cross shows that the writer does not mind taking orders. The shaping of the word 'so' like '50' shows that he is familiar with figures.

The round, extended end strokes reveal the ability to deal with people in a friendly and generous way.

Quiz 25

I would consider Example 3 the most suitable applicant.

He is quick (quick writing), active (quick writing, inclination to the right). He is sociable, enthusiastic and likes to get around (slant to the right, broad writing). He is persuasive (broad writing, clearly shaped and spaced words).

Quiz 26

The writer of Example 3 is the only suitable candidate.

Example 1 (slow, vulgar, greedy) and Example 2 (odd in every respect, see the large breaks inside words) are both out of the question.

But Example 3 (round, small, clear, neat, well-connected, regular writing with extending end strokes) shows a kind, friendly, intelligent, modest and generous person and a neat and reliable worker.

Quiz 27

Example 1 is American (size, lack of pressure, shaping of the capital *I*).

Example 2 is French (shaping of the *M*, roundness, Continental 7).

Example 3 is Central European (angular, slant to the right, different proportions).

Example 4 is British. This you should know.

Quiz 28

Example 1 is a painter. Note the colourfulness of the strokes.

Example 2 is a great soldier. Clear disciplined writing which shows ambition and persistence.

Example 3 is a poet. Fine, simplified, very tasteful writing, with elegant last stroke of *d* showing contemplativeness and openness to sensual perceptions.

Example 4 comes from a gentleman whose hobby is archery. It clearly depicts an arc.

Example 5 comes from an actress. It shows a person who is used to having large space for the development of her personality. It reveals wide and sweeping gestures.

Example 6 is the writing of a dictator. Look at the megalomania of the capital letters, at the actor-like gestures and the elaborated underlining of his signature and personality.

Example 7 comes from a musician. The *i* and *t* look more like musical notes than like letters.

Quiz 29

The easy and natural flow of the writing of Examples 1 and 3 gives no reason for suspecting ill health.

Compare with it the weak pressure, the trembling features and the peculiar ornamentation of Example 2; the heavy pressure, the notched, indented stroke and striking irregularity and illegibility, also the strange starting strokes of Example 4; finally, the smudgy, retouched, slow drawing and the dropping line of Example 5.

Quiz 30

I am sorry we must advise the landlady to inform the police. We hope the gentleman is still alive, but the possibility of a suicidal attempt cannot be ruled out.

The discrepancy between capitals and small letters shows a great discrepancy between ambitions and real fulfilment.

The right slant indicates excitability.

The sharpness and angularity of the writing is an indication of resentment and a certain hardness which may be directed against the writer himself.

The high degree of connection shows fanaticism and the kind of logic which pursues matters to the bitter end.

The pressure of the stroke, especially the dotting of the *r* and *S*, shows that the writer lives under great tension.

The little hooks (*H* and *y*) denote sulkiness.

The straight downstrokes and the lack of endstrokes reveal fatalism and the capacity to break off relations suddenly and abruptly.

The signature, pushed to the left, is commonly regarded as a sign of great disappointment and suicidal tendencies.

The forming of the *H* is uncanny. A purely intuitive graphologist would insist that there is an appearance of gliding into an abyss in this strangely-formed letter and that its second part looks like a human body falling downwards.

Quiz 31

When he came to power Mussolini dropped the Benito completely. His signature became a mere rubber stamp.

He changed his style from a forward slant, indicating an enthusiastic, impatient, aggressive nature to upright writing, showing greater self-confidence, condescension and self-isolation.

He increased the size of his signature greatly, showing the growth of his grandiose conception of himself.

Quiz 32

Very good, dear parents, that you came to see me. Warn your son, as strongly as you can, against this woman, who shows one of the worst characters I have ever seen.

The smudgy, dirty writing, with plenty of dots, arcade connection, with one stroke covering the other, the leaving out of parts of letters, the brutal pressure, the uncanny loop of the *g*, looking like a bloodstained knife, show that this person is a brutal slave of her instincts, a liar, a crook and a fraud, and that she would get away with murder.

A certain quick intelligence makes her only more dangerous.

Quiz 33

A marriage between these two people would be a failure from the start. They are too different.

Look at size and spacing, at the angle of writing and at the form of connection (garland in No. 1, arcade in No 2).

Their personal experiences of space, their social inclinations, their personal ways of adjustment to life and society are completely incompatible, and will never agree together.

Quiz 34

This is a very generous person. The roundness, the size, the broadness and the long, round, extended endstrokes all point to generosity.

Quiz 35

This doodling was done by Edward Stettinius, a recent U.S.A. Secretary of State, during an international conference. Its sharp, forceful strokes indicate a fighter. The small hooks show perseverance and obstinacy.

Quiz 36

Scribble 1 shows intelligence. Notice how imaginatively the

page is filled up and how cleverly this little girl avoided mingling the lines. Every line goes from start to finish without a break.

There is dexterity, imagination, logic and perseverance in this scribble.

The line droops but works up again. It shows that the child is given to fatigue, but also that she has the power of recovery.

It may be a warning to the parents not to let her overwork herself when she becomes persistent, and to give her rest and leisure.

Scribble No. 2 shows that the writer is very backward. Everything is mixed up, with the strokes all criss-cross, and there is no sense or reason anywhere.

Quiz 37

The slight pressure shows that this is a fine and soft, even slightly sensitive personality, rather than a vigorous and pushing one. The static character of the sketches confirm that this is a calm, reasonable personality, slow and phlegmatic, rather than a dynamic and ambitious one. But the regularity of the shading indicates that there is a healthy co-ordination and control of movements.

The choice of motifs shows that the writer's interests lie more in hard work, in the material and technical, in forms and structures, in flowers and animals, than in the purely social and human world. There is good attention to detail and a dry sense of humour.

The sense of form is indicative of good manners and a pleasant, though independent, calm, phlegmatic and perhaps somewhat monotonous approach to others. But the variety of pictures shows that the author has a considerable breadth of interest.

The lightness of the strokes indicate that although the author likes ornaments and soft colours, he dislikes strong colours and everything shrill and loud.

The clear distinction between the individual drawings shows a sense of distinction and discrimination.

Quiz 38

All these children are difficult.

The exaggerated size of Example 1 shows the boaster, who lacks a sense of proportion.

The trembling strokes of Example 2, and the fact that the writer frames his words, that all the *a's* and *d's* are knotted and drawn twice, show a degree of secretiveness and unconscious fears, also of lack of firmness, which should be carefully watched.

The backwardness in the writing of Example 3 is obvious; so are the neurotic amendments and retouching.

Quiz 39

It is Example 2. The stroke is firmer than those of the others, there are neither lapses nor amendments. The writing is regular in height and in distance between letters and words, and in the angle, which is firm and upright. In spite of that some of the letters of this six-year-old boy, like the *h*, show already an original and personal design.

Quiz 40

Goering drew this doodle during his trial at Nuremberg. It shows various technical structures. But prominent is a weird image of a gallows.

You find the picture of a gallows quite frequently in doodles and signatures of men who are on trial or already convicted.

The signature of Heath, the strangler, a few days before he was executed, shows such a picture of a gallows very clearly.

Quiz 41

There was once a discussion among German graphologists as to the meaning of the mixing of the German and the Latin alphabet in the same man's handwriting. One section of the graphologists interpreted it as an indication of a self-taught and self-made man. Another larger section thought it indicated an adventurer and potential criminal. In Hitler's case both interpretations are correct.

The writing shows the uninterrupted flow of fanaticism, with a logical consequence which makes no pause before anything.

The ornamental vertical strokes in the *f* of the second signature, as well as in the *H*, prove the presence of personal taste in every human expression. This arrogant and vulgar little ornament is very similar to Hitler's ornamental little moustache.

Finally, is the tragic curve of the line not like a picture of rise and fall? Note the enterprise and vigour of the start and the morbid weakness and depression at the finish.

Again, as in Mussolini's handwriting, the increase in styles in the second signature and the shortening of the christian name reveals the changes effected by the rise to power.

BOOKS USED

In English

ROSA BAUGHAN. *Character Indicated by Handwriting.* L. Upcott Gill

H. J. JACOBY. *Self-Knowledge Through Handwriting.* J. M. Dent & Sons

JEROME J. MEYER. *P's and Q's.* Geoffrey Bles

R. SAUDEK. *The Psychology of Handwriting.* Allen & Unwin

In French

J. CRÉPIEUX-JAMIN. *Traité Pratique de Graphologie.* Flammarion

J. CRÉPIEUX-JAMIN. *Les Ecritures de Canailles.* Flammarion

E. DE ROUGEMONT. *La Graphologie.* Marcel Riviere

H. SAINT-MORAND. *Les Bases de l'Analyse de l'Ecriture.* Vigot Frères

de la ROCHETIÈRE et LANAUD. *Leurs Ecritures—Notre Destin.*
Edition de la Syntographologie

In German

LUDWIG KLAGES. *Handschrift und Charakter.* J. A. Barth

MAX PULVER. *Symbolik der Handschrift.* Orell Füssli

RUDOLPHINE POPPÉE. *Graphologie.* H. H. Weber

H. GERSTNER. *Handschriftendeutung.* Frankh

ANJA und GEORG MENDELSSOHN. *Der Mensch in der Handschrift.*
Seemann